DISCARD

THE
UNSTOPPABLES

THE
UNSTOPPABLES

TAPPING YOUR ENTREPRENEURIAL POWER

BILL SCHLEY

FOREWORD BY
GRAHAM WESTON

WILEY

Published by John Wiley & Sons, Inc., Hoboken, New Jersey.
Published simultaneously in Canada.

Library of Congress Cataloging-in-Publication Data:

Schley, Bill, 1952-
    The unstoppables : tapping your entrepreneurial power / Bill Schley.
       pages cm
    Includes index.
       ISBN 978-1-118-45949-2 (cloth); ISBN 978-1-118-52627-9 (ebk); ISBN 978-1-118-52621-7 (ebk);
          ISBN 978-1-118-52619-4 (ebk)
    1. Entrepreneurship.   2. Creative ability.   I. Title.
    HB615.W474 2013
    658.4'21—dc23

                                                                                      2013000460

Printed in the United States of America

10 9 8 7 6 5 4 3 2 1

TO RACKERS EVERYWHERE

CONTENTS

Contents

CHAPTER 4

How to Master Emotional Mechanics Like the Experts
57

PART II

Getting Down to Business: Your UnStoppable Tool Kit
69

CHAPTER 5

School of Everything You Need to Know (in an Hour)
71

CHAPTER 6

The Big Picture in an Hour: Ideas, People, and Execution
79

FOREWORD

A Quest for the Essence of Entrepreneurship

THE UNSTOPPABLES ISN'T JUST A BOOK. It's the product of a quest—a shared quest by author Bill Schley and me to discover the keys to entrepreneurship and to share them with people all over America. Our goal is to double the number of entrepreneurs in our country—starting with you, our readers. And if you choose the entrepreneurial path, we want to double your chances of success. Those are the goals behind every chapter and every page of Bill's book.

To understand this objective and why we're so passionate about it, you need to know a little bit about us.

The company I helped found, Rackspace, was launched by three former college buddies from Trinity University in San Antonio, Texas, in 1998. We now employ more than 5,000 Rackers in locations from Texas to London to Hong Kong. Our mission: To provide hosting and cloud computing backed by "Fanatical Support" to more than 200,000 customers worldwide, including most of the *Fortune 100*.

Our world headquarters is located in a building we call the Castle—a once-abandoned mall in a forgotten neighborhood in San Antonio. My desk sits beside the space once occupied by Gingiss Formal Wear, where I rented my first baby-blue ruffled tuxedo for the high school prom. All the experts said we were crazy when we moved here, but I guess that's how we do things at Rackspace: we listen to our Rackers and to our customers first. Only later do we check with the experts.

Today, customers come from all over the world to visit us in this 1.2-million-square-foot space that no one else wanted. They sense the energy of the place, they see the excitement and enthusiasm on every Racker's face, and they tell us that it still feels like a startup— a vibrant enterprise driven by hungry entrepreneurs. Rackspace has evolved into a big, well-managed company that's traded on the New York Stock Exchange, grew by more than 25 percent in 2012 to $1.3 billion in annual revenue, and is earning accolades worldwide— but we've never lost our entrepreneurial zeal.

Maybe that's why *Fortune* magazine just named us one of the Best Companies to Work For in America for the fifth time in six years. People love working here, and we love them back. And in turn we all love our customers. Call another company and you'll probably listen to a recording, start pressing buttons, and listen to more recordings. Call Rackspace and you'll speak with a Racker, trained and empowered to solve our customers' problems. We're famous for our combination of innovative technology and passionate Rackers, which enables us to deliver the Fanatical Support for which we've become known throughout our industry.

You may be starting to get a feeling for why I'm such a believer in the power of entrepreneurship. I've seen it work its creative magic here at Rackspace. I've seen the value it's created for every Racker, for our far-flung customers, and for communities like the one in which our headquarters is located in San Antonio, where our arrival helped reverse 20 years of decline. I know that this same power is what communities all over America need to thrive in the twenty-first century— and I also know, sadly, that it's what far too many are lacking.

That's the source of the obsession that underlies *The UnStoppables*.

My obsession with uncovering insights into entrepreneurship was spurred by the Great Recession of 2008–2009 and the period of sluggish growth that followed. The U.S. job creation engine is broken. How can we fix it? The key is entrepreneurship.

No one works harder to understand entrepreneurship better than the Kansas City, Missouri–based Kauffman Foundation, which bears the name of a great twentieth-century entrepreneur, Ewing Marion Kauffman, a former salesman who went on to found a great pharmaceutical company. I encourage readers of Bill's book to visit the Kauffman Foundation website and dig into its impressive archive of original research, particularly the 2009 report, *The Anatomy of an Entrepreneur*. Recent research by the foundation has shown that the vast majority of new jobs in this country are created by young organizations, those that are less than five years old. Politicians, reporters, and many average citizens tend to assume that job creation is the province of giant corporations—the Fords, GEs, and Walmarts of the world. They do play their part. But the real source of most well-paid, emotionally rewarding jobs is young businesses—and that means entrepreneurship.

So where will the great entrepreneurs of tomorrow come from?

In search of an answer, I visited my alma mater, Texas A&M, where I was invited to speak to their MBA students. They were a bright, idealistic, and engaged bunch. After offering a few remarks, I asked the students, "How many of you would like to start your own businesses one day, or work for a young business?" Practically every hand shot up.

Then I asked, "And how many of you will be doing that as soon as you graduate from A&M?" There were a few chuckles around the room, and nearly all the hands came down. It seems there was a huge gap between the dream of entrepreneurship and the real-life plans most students had created.

I asked the students to explain the gap, and the answers were revealing. Several students pointed to the huge debt they were carrying after years of expensive undergraduate and graduate-school training. Many would graduate owing $50,000 or more. That burden made them more risk averse than when they began their studies. It discouraged all but the most daring among them from undertaking the personal and financial risk that's inevitable when launching or joining a young company.

Others pointed out that, armed with an MBA from a respected university, they could probably land a six-figure salary from a prestigious, established company that their parents would be proud to mention to their friends. That path would give them security (or so they thought) and enable them to quickly start paying down their student loans. Launching a start-up or joining a young company would mean they'd face a far greater opportunity cost—another factor discouraging entrepreneurship.

The third factor, I came to learn, was the nature of MBA studies themselves. The business students at our great universities learn many useful skills—accounting, finance, organizational dynamics, human resource management, and much more. They leave school well equipped to help run mature enterprises. But they don't learn how to assert their will or overcome their fear of failure. And they don't spend enough time studying the essence of entrepreneurship: getting in motion, building your team, and learning how to succeed with customers.

Combining these factors, it's no wonder that entrepreneurship is flagging in America, and that our once-powerful job creation engine is stalled. The educational institutions that we rely on are inadvertently stifling the entrepreneurs who might otherwise emerge. They destroy more entrepreneurial spirit than they create.

I decided that I wanted to try to help solve this problem. And that's where author and branding strategist Bill Schley enters the picture.

I often listen to books on tape while driving to work and back. A few years ago, I happened across Bill Schley's book, *Why Johnny Can't Brand*. The book had made a Top Five Marketing Books of the Year list someone had sent me, and once I heard it, I knew why. It was full of insights that I wanted to put into action.

I reached out to Bill at his offices in Connecticut. A few months later, I welcomed him and his business partner to Rackspace for a tour of our company and some working sessions with our senior leadership team. Bill and I hit it off from the start, and over the ensuing months a business relationship developed into friendship.

Most important, we discovered our mutual passion for entrepreneurship. We were obsessed by the same questions: What lies at the heart of entrepreneurship? Why do some entrepreneurs succeed while others fail? And how can our society double the number of new entrepreneurs we produce?

Bill and I decided to set out on a journey to answer these questions.

Our quest took us well beyond the boundaries of the business world. We journeyed from Texas to New York to the West Coast. From there we traveled to Israel, a tiny nation with an amazing entrepreneurial culture that is well documented in the book *Start-up Nation* by Dan Senor and Saul Singer. We met a host of amazing business founders there, along with government officials, educators, and experts who helped us understand how Israeli society has been reshaped deliberately to foster the spirit of entrepreneurship—with incredible results.

After we returned from Israel, I had to get back to work at Rackspace, but Bill traveled on to Virginia Beach and San Diego, where he observed and met with members of the U.S. Navy SEALs. In his research, he'd discovered that this most elite force of warriors has a number of crucial characteristics in common with the greatest entrepreneurs, including a willingness to adapt on the fly, dedication to the mission, readiness to tackle (and master) risk, and single-minded devotion to the team. He suspected that if he could learn what propels the SEALs beyond all normal human limits to succeed in some of the world's most challenging environments, he might unearth secrets that could fuel the work of aspiring entrepreneurs. And that suspicion proved to be absolutely correct—as you'll learn in the pages of this book.

Finally, our quest brought Bill and me back to where we started—to Rackspace. As I've explained, Rackspace is no ordinary company. We've kept the entrepreneurial feeling alive even as we've gone global. Rackers are as fired up about the mission—to give Fanatical Support to our customers—as we were when we were a start-up.

The question was: How did Rackers accomplish this? Did we really know? If there were definable insights into our success that could help more entrepreneurs succeed as we did, could we codify and explain them? I had to know the answer—in part, for the benefit of our own expanding legions of Rackers. It's critical for us at Rackspace to keep replicating our own success as we grow. Being able to communicate our approach in clear, simple language would be enormously valuable in helping nurture the Rackspace of the future.

At the same time, I knew that countless other Americans could benefit from a deeper insight into the wellsprings of entrepreneurship.

A few years ago, San Antonio Mayor Julián Castro, one of the most dynamic young political leaders in our country, asked me to help lead SA2020, his long-range strategic initiative for the city. That yearlong experience confirmed my belief that if we are going to change our cities, and thus our country, we can only do it by fostering an entrepreneurial culture. Entrepreneurs create fulfilling jobs, unleash opportunities, take the big risks, build wealth, replace the old with the new, and keep our nation competitive.

This conviction is one reason I recently launched a coworking space for startups called Geekdom in San Antonio. After only a year, it has become one of the country's fastest-growing shared working environments for young entrepreneurs. Within its first year, it grew to be the largest program of its kind in Texas, with more than 500 members working with mentors and energetically coming together to transform ideas into new apps, products, and services. Soon a spinoff program took Geekdom into local high schools and middle schools. We're planting the seeds of entrepreneurship early.

Geekdom also became home to TechStars Cloud, part of the Boulder-based nationwide technology accelerator program.

The San Antonio program is unique, as it is devoted to cloud-related innovation. Young developers and entrepreneurs from around the world are knocking on the door, asking to come here. Our second TechStars class is just beginning, and I can't wait to see what emerges from it—perhaps a future Google or Rackspace. So the personal quest that drove Bill Schley and me to travel the world in search of the essence of entrepreneurship has already started to bear some remarkable fruit along the way.

Bill and I didn't set out to write a book. It was only after we came home from our travels and our many conversations that we realized we had accumulated insights worth sharing. An experienced author, Bill decided to take on the task of writing it down—and that's how *The UnStoppables* was born.

This isn't a book about Rackspace, and it's certainly not a book about me. The observations are often fascinating, but they're in Bill's words, not mine. This book is a manifesto and a guidebook for Americans who want to build something of value and take charge of their own destiny. It's an invitation to you to overcome your doubts and fears and to dare to follow your dreams.

America is the original start-up nation. And the land of Thomas Edison, Henry Ford, Bill Gates, and Steve Jobs is still the world's premier source of entrepreneurial creativity and zeal. We have everything it takes to lead the world into a new age of entrepreneurship—and there's never been a better time than now. The Internet provides access to global markets, and the cloud lets you build your business with less capital than ever before. All we need are more people who are ready to get into motion and take advantage of today's unprecedented possibilities.

America is and must remain the Broadway stage of entrepreneurship—the magnetic hub of creativity and growth that entrepreneurs from India, China, Brazil, and everywhere on earth recognize as the greatest place to seek fame and fortune.

I've always believed that the best way to predict the future is to invent it—and the best way to predict *your* future is to invent it yourself. That's the wisdom entrepreneurs understand and live by.

Ask yourself: Do you want to watch others create and build the future, or do you want to do it yourself? If the idea of stepping into the arena and joining the action excites you, you've come to the right place.

Welcome to *The UnStoppables*.

—Graham Weston,
Chairman and Cofounder of Rackspace
San Antonio, Texas

THE UNSTOPPABLES IN SEVEN SENTENCES

1. The war for the future is happening now. It's about jobs and economic power, and we need a wartime response.
2. The key to winning is in the hands of UnStoppable entrepreneurs. We need millions more.
3. We went looking for the essence of entrepreneurship, but we couldn't find the solution in the usual places . . . so we went on a journey.
4. We talked to Israeli entrepreneurs and Navy SEALs—experts in fear, risk, and failure.
5. We found the system nations use in wartime:
   - Distill the *essence* of what it takes to put people in motion, and
   - Teach the *emotional mechanics* of getting started and keeping on through risk.

6. It's called *Accelerated Proficiency*. It makes people believers and makes them UnStoppable.

7. This book is about accelerated proficiency for entrepreneurs. It will

    • debunk the false myths about entrepreneurs and what they do;
    • demonstrate the skills, rules, and power that make entrepreneurs UnStoppable; and
    • show why it works in big companies, too—and why it's the key to the future.

INTRODUCTION

How the Chairman of Rackspace, Some Navy SEALs, and a Few Israeli Innovators Came Together and Discovered the Heart of Entrepreneurship

IT WAS A WARM OCTOBER DAY in Tel Aviv in 2011. Graham Weston and I were sitting in a coffee shop, being entertained by Yossi Vardi, one of the fathers of the entrepreneurial miracle in this tiny country that likes to call itself "Start-Up Nation."[1] Among dozens of tech companies he has seeded, Vardi may be best known for funding ICQ, as in "I Seek You," the Internet instant messaging program developed by his son, who hadn't gone to college, and two others. ICQ had 12 million users by the time AOL bought it in 1998 for

---

[1]Start-Up Nation—term popularized by the superb book by that title.

I

$407 million dollars. If you remember, 12 million users was a lot back in 1998.

Graham and I weren't getting a word in edgewise in the conversation, but we didn't care—we were listening to a guy who'd done more successful start-ups than most first-world countries, waxing poetic with statements like "Business plans and sausages are alike—only people who don't know how they are made will eat them." And "God created the world in six days because he didn't have a customer base" (a back-handed reference to the barriers to innovation that big companies face). As Vardi expounded on the biggest obstacle to entrepreneurship—a syndrome he dubbed "middle manager disease"—he called on the young man who was mopping the floor by our table to illustrate a couple of points.

"The founders at the top of the company still believe in the mission—it's their baby. So do the people down on the floor." (Vardi pointed to the floor mopper.) "They take personal pride in the job and the work they do. By the way, this whole country is on an entrepreneurial mission—even that kid with the mop will be working on one. Watch."

Yossi called over the 21-year-old floor mopper, then the 22-year-old waitress. He asked them whether, besides this job, they were working with their friends to start a company. Both instantly smiled and nodded—and the floor mopper promptly launched into his investor pitch!

What struck us at that moment was a really simple idea. These kids believed, "My ideas can matter. I can dream and I can dare. *It's possible for me.*"

At all levels of society, in schools and even the army, a national culture was teaching them to go ahead and try—and, if they failed, to try again better the next time.

When people feel this way, a kind of switch goes off inside them. They're suddenly inclined to put themselves into motion, to leave the safety of the comfort zone and go for whatever they want to accomplish in life, especially a goal like entrepreneurship. When you get this kind of belief, it makes you UnStoppable.

How you get it is the central theme of this book. It's why we begin our story about American entrepreneurship here at this café in the heart of Israel, talking with a guy whose investment strategy is simply to find and bet on inspired people—regardless of what their business plans look like.

But why should we care about entrepreneurship?

The answer is simple: because entrepreneurs will make the jobs, invent the industries, create the new markets, and populate the big new companies that will lead us to victory in the war for the economic future. They always have. And if we remember who and what we are as a nation, they always will.

Because America is the *original* Start-Up Nation. For more than two centuries, we have been "the place where the future happens first." Not because America was always first in school subjects like reading, physics, and math, or in metrics like military might. We weren't. But we were always first and best in the field we invented. Our unique global asset was dreaming + doing. We are the Entrepreneurs.

In fact, entrepreneurship is literally in our DNA. Every settler had to take a risk and a leap of faith just to get here. They were adventurers, strivers, freethinkers, and dreamers who all came imagining a better life. If you wanted a business or a farm, then you had to start it. And when this entrepreneurial hothouse needed a government, we created disruptive, game-changing systems and institutions that have favored entrepreneurship ever since.

In time, entrepreneurial leadership brought us economic, military, and moral leadership. But now we are in danger of losing it, and if we do, the world as we and everyone else knows it will change.

Today, America's leadership is being disrupted by new competition powered by technology, population, and the universal desire to share the dream America invented. We want the world to enjoy such progress. But to remain leaders, we need to "disrupt back," to be creative and innovative—*entrepreneurial*—in how we advance. The status quo won't get us there.

ENTREPRENEUR PROBLEM, ENTREPRENEUR SOLUTION

When Graham and I launched our search for the secret to creating entrepreneurs, we looked everywhere "inside the box" for the answer.

We talked to countless experts, hoping for an "a-ha! moment" of inspiration and recognition—but that moment refused to come.

We found that professors and business experts had done tons of research and written copious amounts on the subject of entrepreneurship. The problem was that nobody agreed on anything. Their claims were cancelling each other out. The other problem was that they were often writing epiphanies that sounded like this:

> Entrepreneurship is an approach to management defined as the pursuit of opportunity without regard to resources currently controlled and the motivation to pursue those opportunities to achieve a desired future state.

We didn't know what a kid with an idea for a new app, or a mom with a mortgage whose job just went to India, was supposed to do with advice like that.

And then there was the problem of scale.

To compete in the next century, we don't need hundreds or thousands of new entrepreneurs—we need millions. But the current establishment won't provide them. Our educational system is designed to create great Optimizers—people who are really good at maximizing profits, squeezing out inefficiencies, and building best practices—important, even essential, skills. But entrepreneurs specialized in a different set of skills: judging when the rules need to be broken, when to accept risk, and how to keep going in uncharted waters. These are the skills this book will focus on.

Besides that, higher education is getting too exclusive. The best MBA programs cost $100,000 or more and take two years to complete. There are other new programs, like the Silicon Valley–style incubators that offer an amazing, accelerated opportunity to a select number of applicants who are entrepreneurs to start with, drawn from the one or two percent of the population that seem to have the entrepreneurial DNA to begin with. But these programs alone just aren't enough.

We need to tap into our other 98 percent to boost our front-line entrepreneurial force. We need a national mobilization of people, production, and smart government partnership to promote a broader entrepreneurial culture. We realized that we had to look beyond the status quo to figure out how to make it happen. We'd have to find the a-ha! moment for ourselves.

So we went on a journey—a journey to destinations we never anticipated.

────────

OUR ROAD TRIP

One of our first stops was the nation of Israel. It has barely seven million people—2 percent of the U.S. population—yet it's second only to America in its number of venture-funded start-ups, more than all of Europe combined, according to *Start-up Nation*. Twenty years ago, its start-up economy didn't even exist. What happened? We had to find out.

We also went Silicon Valley, Boulder, Colorado, Boston and New York, and the United Kingdom. We spoke with Harvard professors, business legends, rising stars, venture capital moguls, grandfathers from the Greatest Generation—and we *re*-rented *The Karate Kid*. Pursuing our hunch that we might gain fresh insights about overcoming obstacles and succeeding under stress from people who do it for a living in some of the most dangerous locations on earth, we sought out the world's most elite warriors, the U.S. Navy SEALs and their counterparts in the Israeli Defense Forces (IDF).

The journey was long, circuitous, and filled with surprises. But we found what we were looking for.

────────

THE BIG A-HA!'S

Most of what we discovered about what makes ordinary people UnStoppable didn't come from business or academic experts. The best stuff was taught to us personally by members of the SEALs and the Israeli Special Forces. These folks—the toughest and most elite practitioners of risk-management and problem-solving on earth— talk about a key to success that MBA professors don't teach . . . something even more important than the technical mechanics of their craft. They teach what we call *emotional mechanics*—the internal capacity to get yourself started, to keep going, to overcome obstacles, and to innovate on the fly. They are the real-world PhDs in the art and science of making ordinary people UnStoppable— and the lessons they teach apply to anyone who seeks success in any field.

We also discovered a system that can speed up the learning curve for entrepreneurs. It's a set of rules and principles that teaches you how to get into motion, safely and quickly, to accomplish any objective you have. It's called *Accelerated Proficiency*, and it's a system that people have used for centuries to mobilize and train themselves in times of war or crisis. It relies most of all on discovering the essence of whatever challenge you face.

A commander in the IDF explained it like this: "When you are in a tough spot and you have to improvise to save the mission, there is one question you must constantly ask yourself: *Where is the center?*"

It's the question that gets you to the heart of the matter. How do we align this? What is the *essence* of this problem and its solution?

The more you look, the more you see that there is an essence to every important skills-based challenge human beings undertake. The moment we get it, we switch from uncertainty to understanding, from doubt to belief, both mentally and physically.

Take swimming. The best classroom teacher in the world can talk to you endlessly and brilliantly about the theory and concept of swimming. He can spend weeks on the physics of buoyancy, swimming case histories, even take you to the beach to observe it firsthand. You'll know a lot about swimming.

But you'll never understand it—what it is to *do* it—until you jump off the pier and *get wet*. Even just once. Five minutes of thrashing around, getting water up your nose, feeling the cold, controlling the panic, and keeping your head above water is worth five years in that classroom—because those minutes expose you to the essence. And experiencing the essence gives you the emotional ability to starting jumping in and swimming on your own.

Learners can become rapidly proficient at astonishing things when they are soaked in the essence from the start, then given a small skills set and rules set that support the essence. When these elements are tied together, the result is Accelerated Proficiency. Those who aren't exposed to these things, even with years of instruction, may never become proficient at all.

This book is going to show you the essence of entrepreneurship. Then we'll review the short skills and rules sets that will enable Accelerated Proficiency in any enterprise. Some of the insights we'll share may come as a shock to you—a paradigm-shifting "a-ha! moment" that may change your life.

When Einstein first proposed his theory of relativity a century ago, he said, in effect: "All the laws of physics are great, except for two things: We've got light and gravity wrong."

Einstein's pronouncement changed everything, and modern physics was the result.

The institutions teaching entrepreneurship today have got light and gravity wrong. The essence of entrepreneurship is really something quite different from what they believe—and it's the one thing they don't teach.

You'll learn it here. And you may find the impact life-transforming.

PART I: BIG IDEAS ABOUT YOU

Before we take the plunge into the heart of our story, let's take a moment to outline what you can expect as you read the pages that follow. Part I of this book will:

1. Debunk the misperceptions about what an entrepreneur is and who can be one.

2. Introduce Accelerated Proficiency with its simple component parts: the *Skill Set*, the *Rules Set*, and *the Power Set*.

- The Skill Set and the Rules Set provide a few master principles—the kinds of insights countless business veterans say, "we wish we'd known 20 years ago."
- The Power Set is your emotional ability to step up and actually *do it* in the face of risk and uncertainty.
3. You'll get an Emotional Mechanics Crash Course so you can understand how the Power Set works.

With Part I in hand, you'll be ready to go to work.

PART II: YOUR UNSTOPPABLE TOOL KIT

The world's best practitioners can think on their feet. One of their secrets is that they constantly refer to a small set of master principles—what one SEAL called his mental tool kit.

There are two main things we brought back from our journey to the heart of entrepreneurship. The first is a belief in the essence. The second is a unique tool kit for entrepreneurs based on our experiences, our observations, and the phenomenal success of Rackspace—a set of practical principles that work directly with Accelerated Proficiency and are ready for you to use on day one.

Part II lays out a summary of six master aligning principles—keys to success you can carry with you anywhere—that could only be compiled after our worldwide journey. They're based on hours of one-on-one discussions, analysis, and brainstorming about how Rackspace has outpaced nearly all of its competitors while remaining entrepreneurial and remarkably happy. They aren't official Rackspace company positions—they are the author's summary of what he learned from studying the company and talking endlessly with its remarkable chairman and cofounder.

Maybe six big principles don't sound like a lot. But the fact is that the best entrepreneurs in the world can tell you everything they know about business in about an hour. The rest is the intuition they can't articulate—lessons they learned by experiencing successes and failures, things they know without knowing how they know.

You'll learn these lessons too as soon as you get into motion and start practicing the right principles, just as they did.

———

PART III: CONCLUSION: *US*

No one ever succeeds alone. Our nation needs to build a much broader *entrepreneurial ecosystem*, just as drivers need a highway system, carmakers, and gas stations to run their vehicles.

One key part of the ecosystem involves a new kind of company that will maintain its entrepreneurial energy no matter how big it gets—because it's built and led by entrepreneurial DNA—and is dead set on staying that way.

These are the *E-companies*. Today, Rackspace and a few others are prototype E-companies, to the benefit of their engaged employees, enthused customers, and shareholders. America's companies have the unique opportunity and responsibility to help build the entrepreneurial ecosystem. We'll examine how and why.

———

THE POWER THAT'S WAITING

We spent time with special warfare experts in the course of this project so we could apply their emotional wisdom for businesspeople, including ourselves. But at times we wondered whether all the military metaphors would seem irrelevant or even off-putting to a mainstream audience.

Our answer came in a typically cogent response one day from an IDF elite forces commander. He said:

We're not trying to make them into fighters.

We're trying to make them into believers.

That pretty much says it all. Belief isn't a talent or an educational advantage. It's the unblocker of human power, and power is what this is all about. The leader who said this knew it from a career of overcoming obstacles with extraordinary teams of ordinary individuals under the worst kinds of stress. And he didn't mean the irrational, unhinged kind of belief. He meant the rational, confident, competent kind.

Belief channels the power that is born inside every one of us; the ultimate national resource if we are willing to tap it.

Belief starts when we get an eyewitness look at the real barriers, the fears and doubts that hold us back, and the depth of our own power to overcome it. It enables us to take the first step and start feeling the essence.

As Graham would say, "Employees in Entrepreneurial companies begin to believe when they feel like a valued member of a winning team on an inspiring mission—when their work gives them a chance to touch greatness." Such missions are built in places where the entrepreneur's vision is kept alive each day, places that lead members based on their strengths rather than trying to squelch their weaknesses.

Today we need to liberate every ounce of power and belief we've got. We need entrepreneurship in companies ranging from small start-ups to major corporations. It will change how employees think about their careers and how employees and customers are managed. It will shift the center in capitalism to what we would call Human Capitalism.

This book exposes and explores the secrets of starting and staying on that most vital and rewarding of paths—that of the entrepreneur—and how those who succeed at unblocking their entrepreneurial power become the UnStoppables.

━━━━━━

A WORD ABOUT LANGUAGE

As we've explained, this book originated in a journey of discovery shared by author Bill Schley and Rackspace Chairman Graham Weston. But the language and descriptions throughout are Bill's work, except in those places where Graham is quoted by name. The editorial "we" and "us" used in presenting the argument refers to all of us, author and readers, who are exploring the nature of entrepreneurship together. We hope you enjoy the process.

- The Entrepreneurs will make the jobs and create our future.
- America is the original Start-up Nation. We need to mobilize a national effort to double the number of entrepreneurs.
- Academic degree programs miss the essence of entrepreneurship—the emotional mechanics—and they're not geared for Accelerated Proficiency.
- We can find this essence via experts in fear, risk, failure, and success under stress—like the SEALs and the IDF.
- Our entrepreneurial approach combines the rules and tools, powered by the essence, to create Accelerated Proficiency
- The Entrepreneurs are complemented by the Optimizers. We need to recognize and honor both.

Take the power of believing. Accept that fear, risk, and failure are vital for achieving. This makes people UnStoppable.

PART I

Big Ideas About You

1

Who Is an Entrepreneur and What Do They Do, *Really*?

WE NEED TO NAIL DOWN OUR DEFINITION of *entrepreneur* right now or our plane will never leave the gate. There are as many definitions as there are books, blogs, and helpful aunts. But they seldom agree and they set false expectations, and that stops a lot of people from starting.

The number one myth is that you need to be a genius like Steve Jobs, or a visionary who goes around all day seeing things that others don't see, or a lone rider control freak who either has to be CEO or nothing, or a daredevil who basks in risk. People also believe all entrepreneurs must have access to a financial stash that others don't (such as venture capital—VC—investment money), have some specialized knowledge or education, and start with a complete, fail-safe plan that's guaranteed to succeed.

That's all wrong—by around 180 degrees.

Most people are startled by the findings that author and professor Amar V. Bhide uncovered in one of the most extensive studies on the subject. Bhide explains that the vast majority of start-ups that eventually make it to the *Inc*. 500 list of fastest-growing private companies began like this:

- no new technology or breakthrough idea
- $10,000 of friends and family financing
- little or no formal planning
- opportunistic adaptation instead of vision—that is, they reacted as much as they acted.
- unproven human capital—they weren't experts when they started[1]

In other words, most noteworthy businesses come from completely unremarkable origins. They start their businesses by copying or slightly modifying someone else's idea. Their vision isn't set in the beginning; instead, they adapt it as they learn what works and what doesn't through rapid trial and error. Only an elite few start with VC-type capital funding, and none of them are Bill Gates.[2]

────────

OPINIONS: EVERYBODY'S GOT ONE . . .

Definitions of *entrepreneur* run the gamut. They range from the intellectual, such as this one by Harvard Business School professor Howard Stevenson, who said, "Entrepreneurship is the pursuit of opportunity beyond resources currently controlled," to the homespun and humble, such as this one from Eric Jacobsen, a successful entrepreneur I know: "I've read dozens of books on the subject. They disagree as much as they agree. The only consistent truth we can find that comes up over and over again seems to be this: 'The difference between entrepreneurs and everybody else is: the entrepreneurs are

────────

[1] Amar V. Bhide, *The Origin and Evolution of New Businesses* (New York: Oxford University Press, 2003).
[2] Ibid.

simply the ones that step up to the plate; successful entrepreneurs are the ones that *just keep swinging.*' "

It's the entrepreneurs themselves who always give the most simple, bottom-line definitions for what they do. Eric later told me with a hint of pride, "They give a test in business school with the ten traits that are absolutely essential for an entrepreneur. I only had one."

Different industries skew the definitions, too. Case in point: the high-tech and Internet industries are by nature innovative and iconoclastic or they wouldn't exist. Every business element—the products, the platforms, and the markets themselves—are all moving targets! So definitions of entrepreneurship from people in silicon valley often sound like this: Entrepreneurs are iconoclasts who create a new product or service under conditions of extreme uncertainty.[3]

This definition assumes disruptive new products and scary levels of risk. That would scare lot of folks away from trying—if it were true.

The fact is that many of the best entrepreneurs in the world don't fit this definition. They are *risk mitigators*, not risk lovers. They avoid risks except when absolutely necessary, and rather than producing earth-shaking industry disruptions, they just make small, fundamental changes in a business model that turn out to produce good results. Take McDonald's master builder Ray Kroc, for instance. He didn't purchase his small chain of hamburger stands from the original McDonald brothers under "extreme uncertainty." And he didn't sell a revolutionary product like an iPad that no one had ever seen. He sold burgers. He knew the basic model worked—that people wanted to buy cheap, hot burgers and shakes that were ready in a minute—because the stores he bought had proven it. What he wasn't certain about was how far he could build his idea of automating and systematizing the food-preparation process, or just how fabulously

---

[3] Eric Ries, *The Lean Startup: How Today's Entrepreneurs Use Continuous Innovation to Create Radically Successful Businesses* (New York: Crown Business, 2011).

big McDonald's would grow. That's where his own entrepreneurial contribution came in.

The point is, you may or may not fit into somebody else's neat definition of an entrepreneur. But no one can exclude you or predict your future success or failure. Trust the Navy SEALs on that.

───────

WHO'S GOING TO MAKE IT THROUGH HELL WEEK?

SEAL team instructors know one person can't predict another's heart, mind, and soul, so they don't try. On the first day of training, 119 or so gung-ho, preselected candidates show up on the beach for BUD/S (Basic Underwater Demolition/SEAL) training. Many are star athletes, team captains, and military academy grads—physical specimens right out of *Rambo*. Others are as ordinary looking and undistinguished as the stock room kid at Home Depot. Greeting them are the instructors, all veteran SEALs who pride themselves on having a sixth sense about being able to pick a brother SEAL out from the crowd.

But no instructor ever knows ahead of time who will be the 19 or so left standing about a month later. There's no reliable psychological predictor, no body type, no IQ or background benchmarks. "Doing" itself will be both the teacher and the decider. As the saying goes, "Action is character." The only guarantee is this: If you don't start, you fail. If you quit, you fail. Everything else is up for grabs.

Many of the best entrepreneurs would tell you that entrepreneurship itself is that disarmingly simple: "When all is said and done, when the theories and books are put away, the only difference is that the entrepreneur *did*. And everyone else *didn't*." So says Dan Schley, another successful entrepreneur (who also happens to be a Harvard MBA).

What makes you do or not do, quit or not quit, is the paramount question in *The UnStoppables*—and for you as an achiever of anything. Because nobody knows who will become a successful entrepreneur. But—

HERE'S WHAT WE DO KNOW

Entrepreneurs have a *yearning*. It's simply an unfilled personal need to get something, fix something, find something, do something, experience something, or make something that simply doesn't exist.

Having this unfilled need eats at them and causes anxiety. Anxiety makes them uncomfortable. Being uncomfortable makes them move to change their situation.

Some call this *entrepreneurial anxiety*—but yearning is all it is: a specific dream + desire. And any one will do—as long as it's strong enough to get you in motion, because motion is magic. Psychologists may tell us that anxiety is bad, but a smidgeon of anxiety is a blessing for any entrepreneur.

It can push you or pull you. It can even be totally mundane, as long as it tips your scale. Mark Zuckerberg supposedly started Facebook because he wanted to get girls, not change the whole world.

Graham Weston says he started coming up with ideas for businesses that he could work in because "I thought no one would ever hire me. I thought I'd never be able to excel as an employee. In high school, I wasn't just the last kid to be picked for the team—I wasn't even picked. But I still had this yearning for someone to see I had some potential."

Some entrepreneurs are running toward a dream of riches, power, or fame. Some are running away from a nightmare of poverty, or a disappointing parent, or the fear of not being able to use the gifts they have. Some just dream of owning a business and being the boss.

What all entrepreneurs have in common is the intense drive to satisfy their yearning—and they accept that they'll have to travel through some risk to get there. But the less risk, the better. No successful entrepreneur jumps out of bed each day because they want to play roulette with their personal savings or take risk for its own sake.

There's an interesting parallel here with skydivers. Although most people have never met one, they assume skydivers do it because they love the danger. But a skydiver does it because she yearns to fly, not for a chance to die. She'll say she has a *life* wish, not a death wish. So she's willing to take a managed risk and accept its realities to get where she wants to go—in this case, the sky. The goal is to get the minimum necessary proficiency as fast as possible so she can practice and teach herself to be really good at it.

Whether or not they'd ever jump out of a perfectly good airplane, entrepreneurs have a life wish and accept that there will be obstacles in the path to living it.

. . . AND SO DO MOST FIVE-YEAR-OLDS

Needs, anxiety, dreams, yearning: according to education expert Chris Lehman, all we've described are the magical properties all five-year-olds have.

Chris runs a charter high school in the city of Philadelphia called Science Leadership Academy. He has worked the principles of entrepreneurship into the core curriculum for all grades, and he reminded us that "every five-year-old is a creative inventor." Just watch how they play with their friends. They imagine making something they don't have. They are anxious to get it. They instantly act to put it together with whatever resources they have lying around in the yard or the closet, because they have no Fear, Uncertainty, and Doubt (FUD) to extinguish their dreams and desire.

Education and creativity expert Sir Ken Robinson says that at the age of five, 98 percent of kids score at nearly a genius level for a quality called *divergent thinking*: the capacity to think "laterally," entirely outside the box, to find creative answers to mundane problems. But it drops off precipitously as we advance from age five to grown-up—squelched by our educational system, he says, which tells kids, "There's just one answer, at the end of the book, and don't collaborate—that's cheating." There are millions more of us who are brilliant at thinking divergently but have been told we can't, we shouldn't. Entrepreneurs have just managed to hold on to more of that way of thinking that we all had when we were five-year-old inventors.

It's never been lost, it just needs to be exposed. It's there whether you're five or fifty-five. It just needs to be retapped, like an undepleted oil well.

THE ENTREPRENEUR'S REAL DIFFERENCE

Entrepreneurs are not smarter, savvier, or luckier than anyone else. They have simply mastered the emotional mechanics of *doing*. Not the technical ability to do, or the talent to do, but the decision, the act, and—with practice—the art of doing. So here's a really simple definition of *entrepreneur*:

> Entrepreneurs have an idea, then put themselves in motion to make it reality. They turn ideas into physical value: goods, services, and jobs that weren't there before.

Everyone dreams and talks. Entrepreneurs *do*.

The second sentence of our definition is pivotal: creating value that wasn't previously there. If you want a single sentence about why our world needs entrepreneurs, that's it. An entrepreneur who imagines owning a tennis shop and opens it in a once-vacant space has produced a new entity and an opportunity that wasn't there. An entrepreneurial employee inside a big company who convinces IT to program a new software module for his team to give faster, more personal customer service has fabricated an asset that wasn't there. Entrepreneurs are society's makers of the intangible into the tangible. They literally turn mind into matter. And because it doesn't exist before it's imagined, the value that entrepreneurs add to society originates out of thin air.

WHAT DO THEY DREAM ABOUT?

Where does the opportunity originate in the minds of so many innovators and entrepreneurs? It's the result of a habit they have that anyone can learn, a habit of asking the three or four great entrepreneurial questions whenever their desires are unfulfilled or they're blocked by a process that doesn't make sense:

1. I wish I could, so why can't I?
2. What if?
3. How come no one ever fixed that?
4. Why does this have to be such a pain?

It's remarkable how easy it is to ask these questions, and the more you do, the more often you respond with commonsense answers that *no one has ever thought of*. There seldom is anything profound about these answers, just a need and an unsatisfied individual. And if other people happen to share this need, successful entrepreneurial businesses result.

Entrepreneurs distinguish themselves by asking these kinds of questions a lot and by going ahead and actually *doing* things to answer their own questions. Everybody else just talks.

Even many of those who have followed the Rackspace story closely don't realize that Rackspace was originally founded by three web developers, fresh out of college, who just needed more server space. Pat Condon, Dirk Elmendorf, and Richard Yoo wished they could just go to a secure, professionally-run data center and rent the space they needed for their fledgling IT service—a kind of fractional share, the way you can buy time on a private jet. But they couldn't find a service that made sense. They wondered, "Why not?" And because no one else had an answer for their question, they just set up our own. And since there was extra capacity, they decided to see if there were other techies who might like to rent some unused server space like they had wanted to. They did!

Graham met the three founders and, as a young entrepreneur himself, he recognized their potential. They became partners. Today they have more than 200,000 business customers. All because three college kids had the audacity to wonder, "Why not?"

FROM ENTREPRENEUR*IAL* TO ENTREPRENEUR

Yearning + doing makes you *entrepreneurial* at any stage. And that's very important, because it allows you to overcome inertia and get started.

But there is one thing more you must do to earn your wings and call yourself an entrepreneur. Successful entrepreneurs *do + don't quit.*

This doesn't mean you don't try different avenues, fail, regroup, and sometimes halt one effort to reallocate your resources. It just means, as Winston Churchill said, "When you're going through hell, keep going." You persist, you work through the problems and around the obstacles that you know are always on the path to value. You persist because UnStoppable principles and practice make you believe you can. You persist because there is no entrepreneurship without it. Daring and doing always pays dividends.

The entrepreneur keeps swinging until he's achieved some worthwhile value. It is not always the exact value he originally set out to create, because unknowns are revealed along the way. The advantage is seldom in the brilliance of the initial idea, which always morphs and changes in the process. As we'll see, the magic comes through the simple act of putting oneself in motion and adapting as needed.

It'd be a cliché and incorrect to claim that entrepreneurship is for everyone. But millions more can decide to think and act in the entrepreneurial way. A great proportion of those will discover they are entrepreneurs as well. People like you.

It's a numbers game. And we need every one.

BIG WIDE TENT

Chris Lehman made another vital point for us: "People think entrepreneurship and they immediately think business. But entrepreneurship is the idea that people can have powerful ideas, own those ideas and do meaningful things with them. Not just to create a job, but to create a life. Where that leads to businesses, great—where that leads to non-profits or to schools, great. But the core idea is that doing things like we've always done is not going to solve the world's problems in the next 100 years."

Amen.

NOT JUST FOR START-UPS

So if you thought an entrepreneur was an iconoclast who risks it all to invent a whole new category like Cirque du Soleil or Netflix, you'd be right. But you'd be right about only a fraction of the process because entrepreneurship is vital at every one of the following business stages—*not just for start-ups*.

Start-up entrepreneurs find their sweet spot in early-stage organizations. They love the urgent pace, the thrill of takeoff, the close-knit teams, the lack of rules, the sense of mission, and the ability to wear lots of hats and do something no one else has done. They have what it takes to build a business from, let's say, 0 to 50 employees. But they may not have the desire or the skills to manage beyond that size.

Second-stage entrepreneurs have a different but no less important set of skills and affinities. These are the ones that take something small- or medium-sized and make it global—orders of magnitude greater than the founders ever envisioned. They create a lot of jobs as they do.

Donald Trump, Thomas Watson, Jr., Ray Kroc, and Charley Housen didn't start the companies that made them famous. They inherited or bought more modest businesses that were already working. Then they blew open the original model with vision and strategies that were every bit as creative as the company founders'.

Inside entrepreneurs are employees already working within companies or organizations. They have an idea for how to make an improvement, and then they act to make it real. Some would say that these people don't take the kind of existential risks that outside entrepreneurs do. But that depends on where you look. In companies that are run the old-fashioned way—those that punish employee weaknesses instead of managing to their strengths—employees may risk their jobs and reputations to be entrepreneurial. Inside entrepreneurship can flourish in organizations that genuinely feed it and water it—the way Google and 3M, for example, allocate paid work time to their employees to develop personal projects that may or may not produce a financial payoff.

Solo entrepreneurs may not create organizations, but they make a huge collective entrepreneurial contribution nonetheless. They develop networks and generate commerce while supporting households on a broad scale. Don't forget that most titans of industry began as bootstrapping solo entrepreneurs at one point.

Nothing precludes anyone from going all the way from garage to gargantuan, of course. Doing that requires founders committed to the long-term and an extraordinary team. The way Bill Gates and Steve Jobs did it, of course. So did Rackspace founders Richard Yoo, Dirk Elmendorf, Pat Condon, Morris Miller, and Graham Weston. They're not as famous as Bill and Steve perhaps, but then again, you may not have visited Rackspace—yet.

NOT JUST FOR CEOS

People think of CEOs when they hear "entrepreneur," but CEOs are just the tip of the iceberg. There is one commander on any four-person SEAL team, but all four members are warriors. All four are essential for success. All four are at risk. All four must solve a shared set of problems on a shared mission. Responsibility and accountability fall on one and all.

In an entrepreneurial company, the founding team and their key employees are *all entrepreneurs*. There must be a leader, a CEO whose job is to be the constant keeper of the vision, the one main person who focuses on the big and little pictures. But each member takes on entrepreneurial risk and responsibility when they join this team. Each has volunteered to get on the roller coaster and go up or down with it. Each comes to work every day to turn an idea into action.

The same can be true in traditional large companies—if and when entrepreneurial culture is allowed to survive and thrive. Team members who are allowed to ask "What if?," "How come?," and "Why couldn't we?"—who are willing to risk mistakes, discomfort, and failure anxiety to create a value that wasn't there before—are operating as entrepreneurs.

We need 'em all.

WHAT IT ADDS UP TO

"Whatever you do, or dream you can, begin it. Boldness has genius and power and magic in it."

—Goethe

Substitute "motion" or "doing" for "boldness" in that quote and you're on your way.

Through our travels, I did find one reliable predictor for who becomes an entrepreneur that has ramifications for the larger culture of entrepreneurship (which we'll talk about later). The biggest predictor is whether or not you've had direct exposure to entrepreneurs among your family or friends (including mentors) while growing up. Exposure to those to whom you have emotional attachments sets you up with the four tenets of belief, flipping the "It's possible for me" switch at a formative age. (Belief Cultures are described in the following chapters.)

If you haven't had the gift of such exposure, the UnStoppable principles and learning techniques are going to provide it. As you'll learn in Chapter 2, we are going to get you wet.

I hope you're no longer wondering who is or isn't intellectually, educationally, or financially qualified to be an entrepreneur—that you realize that those factors are irrelevant. The key to the kingdom is your ability to simply *do*: to harness emotional mechanics and Accelerated Proficiency to unstop what inhibits you from getting yourself in motion.

Doing pays dividends.

- Entrepreneurs *dream* + *do*. They have ideas and execute them to build new economic value. Everybody else talks. That's the difference.
- Most entrepreneurs are not geniuses or visionaries, despite what the media says.
- Entrepreneurs have a need, a yearning for something better, that causes creative anxiety. They let their desire become stronger than their doubt.
- They ask the simplest "What if?" and "Why not?" questions.
- Everyone can't decide to be brilliant, educated, or clever— but *anyone* can decide to do.
- Don't bemoan your struggles. Your gift is the difficulty you've overcome.
- Doing pays dividends.

2

Accelerated Proficiency

IF OUR TASK IS TO UNLEASH VAST NEW NUMBERS of entrepreneurs, Accelerated Proficiency is at its heart. It's an all-purpose concept that goes against long-standing educational and consulting methodology—an entrepreneurial approach. But new, it's not.

Accelerated Proficiency is what happens whenever the underdog has an acute survival problem and doesn't have the resources, money, people, time, or technology to figure out the answer—just the emotional will to solve it anyway. For example, Accelerated Proficiency is what has happened throughout history when your peace-loving nation is surprise-attacked by a totalitarian power and you have to turn millions of ordinary citizens into superior pilots, soldiers, submariners, and commandos—not to mention convert whole industries into war production—overnight. It is also the approach that has enabled many entrepreneurial companies to survive against an onslaught by far bigger, richer, longer-established, and seemingly better-equipped competitors—and even to sweep up the pieces after their larger rivals ultimately bite the dust.

Accelerated Proficiency runs on two things: a concentrated set of high-yield principles that launch you and keep you on a winning path, and the emotional mechanics to do it, which we'll explain in detail in the Emotional Mechanics Crash Course.

Of all the a-ha! moments we experienced when researching the UnStoppables, perhaps the most important was the realization that you can apply Accelerated Proficiency to *anything*—including our acute national need to mobilize thousands of new, effective entrepreneurs to control our economic future.

WAX ON, WAX OFF

During my research for the book, I re-rented the 1984 movie *The Karate Kid* to see that legendary scene where the old karate teacher makes the Kid, Daniel, wax his car. It makes a game-changing point about learning anything, entrepreneurship included, in the fastest, most frugal[1] way when you're strapped for time and resources—like the Israelis have been for the past two millennia, for example. You find out quickly that it's 100 times better to spend two weeks immersed in the essence, get Minimally Functionally Qualified (MFQ), and start doing it for real, than it is to spend two years studying without the essence.

It's remarkable how many people remember this scene, which is more than 25 years old. Daniel is desperate to learn karate to compete in the local championship against the rich bully, who is also harassing Daniel's girl. The old Japanese janitor in his apartment building—who happens to be a karate master—promises to teach him. Of course, he only has three weeks!

But when the Kid shows up for practice the next day, there's no karate lesson. Instead, the old man takes him out back to his car, puts a wax buffer in his hand, and shows him how to make wide, circular motions with the cloth, back and forth. Left hand, right hand. "Wax on, wax off, Daniel-san," he says. Hours later, he makes him sand the floor and paint the house the same way.

---

[1] Gerd Gigerenzer, *Gut Feelings: The Intelligence of the Unconscious* (New York: Penguin, 2008).

After a couple of days of this, the Kid is flipping out. The teacher tricked him into waxing his car and painting his shed! He's terrified that he's going to get murdered on Saturday. He turns to storm out . . .

But then the master shows him, cutting graceful circles in the air with his hands: "See: Wax on, wax off. Wax on, wax off." It's the perfect karate motion. The essence of every *kata* Daniel needs has been absorbed into muscle memory. He does it without having to think. It's internalized in a custom-fit way. There would never have been enough time for Daniel to learn 100 karate combinations. But he *could* learn a few deep principles from which all balance, speed, power, and everything would become aligned.

The Kid gets the trophy. The audience gets a big life principle. We got one of the central tenets of accelerated learning for this book. (Incidentally, you can search "Karate Kid, Wax on, Wax off" and watch the scene on YouTube. It's still good.)

We discovered later that there's a hugely successful, real-life entity that actually uses the same principles to train hundreds of thousands of people in self-defense, among other critical skills, in an incredibly short amount of time. It's the Israeli Army.

THE KRAV MAGA KIDS

In real life, the martial arts are built on exquisite, technique-driven motions that instill an almost mystical power into the practitioner. It takes years of training to get proficient.

That, of course, doesn't work for the Israelis. Their army has to take teenaged kids of all shapes, sizes, and abilities away from their iPads and turn them into the bulwark of national defense. It doesn't have big budgets and it doesn't have years to work with. It has weeks.

So the Israelis found an entrepreneurial solution. They developed Krav Maga: a super-effective self-defense system that teaches hand-to-hand combat to anyone in about a month.

The approach works because it's not built on a large number of strict techniques and refined motions. Instead, Krav Maga teaches a small number of essential, open principles that the user can apply to a whole variety of situations—for example, always attacking the body's most vulnerable spots, and using your natural instinctive reactions in a fight. The critical thing is that anyone who learns it can become MFQ in a super-accelerated amount of time. From then on, the rest is only practice.

As the manuals warn you right up front, "Krav Maga is not pretty. It leaves art and beauty at the doorstep. It has no rules except what works to keep you alive against an attacker." Krav Maga has a very simple focused mission that never varies—disable your attacker just enough so you can escape with your life. Everything grows out of and comes back to the same few principles. But with those in mind, you learn quickly to think on your feet and adjust to the most unexpected variables. It's exactly what you'll need in combat—not to mention as an entrepreneur.

The Israeli experience with Krav Maga is representative of the approach they've used to solve problems since David with his sling-shot went up against Goliath with his huge size and strength advantage and his giant wooden club. Since their beginnings, Israelis have faced existential threats with no resources, no superiority in numbers, no time to waste, and no allies—and won. Their Krav Maga–like approach to surviving and thriving against the odds points directly to a huge principle for us in our own quest to train a high volume of entrepreneurs, including you, in a smart, fast, inexpensive, and effective way.

ACCELERATED PROFICIENCY 101

Accelerated Proficiency is the art and science of getting people to be Minimally Functionally Qualified (MFQ) in a sharply accelerated time frame so they can get in motion, start doing, and effectively teach themselves, rather than talking and observing. It centers on visualizing, remembering, and practicing the essence, which makes it the key for creating learning programs that scale. Accelerated Proficiency provides you with a Skill Set, a Rules Set, and a Power

Set. These are what enable you to visualize the whole process, get yourself to do it one time on your own, and repeat it at will.

The Skill Set contains the basic elements that you need to perform the function. The Israelis call these your *technicals*. In tennis, it would be how to hold the racquet, hit a forehand or backhand, and serve. In sailing, it's knowing how to pull up the sails, steer with a tiller, and tack.

The Rules Set is a few key heuristics (rules of thumb) to avoid the likeliest hazards and keep you safe enough to come back another day. In sailing, for example, one rule says, "When you're in trouble, point into the wind."

The Power Set is the emotional ability to start and complete the whole sequence without your instructor—for instance, untie the boat from the dock, go out to sea, and come back—more than once. It's the unconscious and conscious belief that "it's possible for me" that lets you flip the go-switch and leave the dock.

Accelerated Proficiency gives you the MFQ to get you in motion so you can start learning all the unconscious things and develop the expert intuition[2] that a seasoned practitioner can't really articulate to you—the things he does automatically, the things he "just knows." His intuition is really not magic; he has simply seen so many cases that after a while he sees patterns that others don't see. He can connect the dots in a flash of insight that others don't have because his unconscious recognizes the connections. He's "been there, solved that." The whole point of Accelerated Proficiency is to get you on the road to this transcendent level of expertise so you can keep on going by yourself, without the help of a teacher.

The Accelerated Proficiency approach to emotional mechanics is handled the same way—starting with understanding and conceptualizing, then physically experiencing the situation to gain a Skill Set, Rules Set, and Power Set. This gives you the tools you need to get started doing just about anything.

Using Accelerated Proficiency principles, we are going to explore the Krav Maga model for entrepreneurship.

---

[2] Daniel Kahneman, *Thinking, Fast and Slow* (New York: Farrar, Straus and Giroux, 2011).

THE FOUR STEPS FOR ACCELERATED PROFICIENCY

We've named the three components needed to achieve MFQ: a Skill Set, a Rules Set, and a Power Set. Whether you are learning a simple skill or the elements of emotional mechanics, you'll need to follow a four-step sequence:

1. *Get It Exposed:* First, bring to light the false facts, assumptions, and hearsay that breed continual Fear, Uncertainty, and Doubt (FUD)—and then remove them. This is why classic military boot camps begin by "breaking recruits down" before building them back up, and why the demystifying "Who Is an Entrepreneur?" is the first chapter of the book.

2. *Get a Snapshot:* Second, develop your ability to picture the essence and understand the sequence of achieving it from beginning to end—quickly and basically. Visualizing the whole process overwhelms intellectual FUD. It lights the spark of "it's possible for me." It gives us permission to believe.

3. *Get Wet:* Third, get completely wet, ASAP. Instead of just studying the essence, you've got to touch it, feel it, and live in it to train your conscious and unconscious in the real thing. Experiential immersion in the essence overwhelms FUD.

4. *Get in Motion:* Last, adhere with a vengeance to a unique variation on the familiar 20:80 rule: Spend 20 percent or less of your time pondering and preparing, and 80 percent or more *doing*—repeatedly.

THE LAW OF MOTION

There is a fitness rule that says simply "Moving heals, sitting kills." Our high school physics teachers told us that one of Newton's three laws of motion is that objects in motion tend to stay in motion; objects at rest stay at rest. A SEAL told me that, in house-to-house combat, moving forward is what keeps you alive.

Getting into motion is how you see where the markets are, where the need is, how the prototypes work, and where the doors will open for you, all of which you can never see from the confines of your comfort zone. Motion presents you with examples, experiences, problems, and solutions, and variations on themes. Motion has been said to cure depression and malaise. It begets momentum. And it introduces you to that all-important factor in business and life: people.

Crucially, forward motion moves you closer to your entrepreneurial vision, and the clearer your vision, the more powerful it is. This is why motion is our first, second, and third law of UnStoppable dynamics. It's why so much of our doctrine is geared directly toward enabling it. In any aspect of your career, never forget the law of motion.

HOW TO DO ANYTHING THE AP WAY

There are a few unbreakable principles that are always required to give yourself Accelerated Proficiency. Use these and they'll make you more effective at anything you do.

Legendary coach Vince Lombardi once told his team before a big game: "Gentlemen, today's football game will be decided by three or four plays. Unfortunately, I don't know which ones they'll be, so you'll have to play them all."

Accelerated Proficiency rules are like that. It turns out *three or four* is the universal constant for learning and applying anything—the prime numbers for planning, breaking down problems, team building, and executing—especially in dynamic environments, which is where entrepreneurial ventures always occur. It has to do with the elemental geometry of triangles and squares. Three points define a plane or the support required from a piano stool. Four points determine everything from a table's legs to the compass quadrant to the four corners of the earth.

You'll learn hundreds of principles throughout your career. But when you're planning and running your mission, you'll default to three or four top-level principles, and these will be the trusted success-makers that you will use to remind yourself, over and over, of what works best.

Likewise, you'll adopt sets of three or four principles for everyday functions—like positioning your brand, prospecting for leads, or bringing your tugboat into a dock. *And that's all you'll need.* "Three or four, no less no more." From here on, always be on the lookout for your magic three or four. Some may jump out at you in a big explosion. But don't overlook the quiet, subtle ones, because they're often the most profound. Remember—a temperature drop of one degree can change the whole world from rain to snow. Home runs win in the movies. But a bunt base hit that rolls thirty feet up the third-base line is often the winning difference in real life.

So now let's consider the three master principles of Accelerated Proficiency.

THINK ON YOUR FEET

Being UnStoppable includes the power to think and innovate on your feet under real conditions in real time. That means carry-on wisdom is what you need. Ask any entrepreneur or SEAL, and they'll tell you that the rules and procedures you can use on the fly are worth 20 times the ones at home in the file. These are the ones you're going to think in the shower with, brainstorm strategies with, synthesize answers in presentations with, and get out of jams with. UnStoppable lessons are compact and portable—one reason the rule of three or four is essential to thinking on your feet.

The best principles to rely on in times of stress are what we call *heuristics*—the mental "rules of thumb" that guide all human decision-making. When survival's on the line, we shift to intuition that is fast and accurate—unconscious intelligence that skips past normal reasoning. We often call this intuition "gut feeling," but it actually comes from the preset rules-of-thumb we carry around wherever we go. Our brains love heuristics because they get us to the heart of the matter on minimal bandwidth, enabling snap judgments that are usually right.

I'd like to say I invented heuristic learning, but I didn't. It's copied from my mother and yours. They used heuristics when they taught us lessons like "Where there's smoke, there's fire," "Look both ways when you cross the street," "Practice makes perfect," and "Honesty is the best policy."

Rules of thumb expressed in nifty little word packages like these are fastest way to learn and remember. These powerful mini word packages are called *Micro-Scripts*, and Accelerated Proficiency is full of them.

Before writing this book, I thought Micro-Scripts were mostly for marketers and political campaigns. The greatest advertising taglines are made from them—lines like "Melts in your mouth, not in your hand," "Friends don't let friends drive drunk," or "A diamond is forever." Then I noticed that the SEALs and the Israeli Maglan special forces also learn this way—and so do pilots and sailors, doctors and world-champion athletes, whose lives or livelihoods depend upon thinking on their feet.

So we constantly condense big principles into heuristics, then pack them in a Micro-Script. "Teach me a lesson, give me a rule." That's the SEAL method of training, soon to be yours.

SIMPLE BEATS COMPLICATED

Peeling back the onion to its core requires us to sacrifice complicating factors that let some people hedge their bets. These factors are the reason that many people who talk about K.I.S.S. (Keep It Simple, Stupid) seldom do it. But simple is the express lane to UnStoppable. Simple beats complicated every time.

The Ten Commandments fit on four and a half lines. The Gettysburg Address runs half a page. The greatest ideas expressed throughout human history—the only ones we remember—are invariably simple and generally brief. So if your business plan is complicated, it isn't a business plan. One of the most legendary venture capitalists from Silicon Valley once said, "The best business plans can fit on the back of a business card." If your Unique Difference can't be explained in that little space, you don't have one yet. If you can't say what it is in a sentence of two, you can't say it.

Remember this when you tell your story, whether in the form of a business plan, a mission statement, or a marketing or investment pitch. There is virtually no idea, no process, no vision that simplicity and brevity can't improve—and never let a bureaucrat, business consultant, or attorney try to tell you otherwise.

———

DEFINE THE CENTER—AND GO ALL IN

Accelerated Proficiency principles always point to the center of any problem, because the center is the place to go all in. UnStoppables wake up every day on a quest to keep the center of their brand, their performance, their culture, or their status as the customers' #1 choice locked in the crosshairs. As any pilot on landing approach knows, it takes constant vigilance to stay lined up. UnStoppables win by going all in where it counts. And nothing counts more than the center.

- Accelerated Proficiency principles can be applied to virtually anything to get the essence and get going—faster, cheaper, and better:
  - AP explains the effectiveness of super-fast, super-accelerated training programs like Krav Maga or learning to fly a plane.
  - AP is what was going on in the "Wax on, wax off" scene in *The Karate Kid*.
  - Entrepreneurship is not an exception.
- Accelerated Proficiency is vital to any war effort, including the one we need now in entrepreneurship.
- Accelerated Proficiency involves three things: a Skill Set, a Rules Set, and a Power Set.
- Accelerated Proficiency gets you MFQ: Minimally Functionally Qualified.
- Your guiding principles should always come down to three or four—no less, no more.
- Accelerated proficiency rules are designed to help you:
  - Think on your feet
  - Use easy rules of thumb
  - Keep it simple
  - Find the center
  - Go all in

3

Emotional Mechanics

What Only Neuroscientists, Your Friends in the SEALs, and the Israeli Army Will Tell You

Fear. Now fear's interesting, it keeps you in your hole. You spend all your time avoiding it. But you never can. So you start a relationship. You let it sit on the seat next to you. You tell it to stay put so you can do your job. Until one day you realize: You're no good without it. It gives you your power, your edge, your game. The fear you thought was stopping you is making you *UnStoppable*. And that's the most powerful thing of all.

— *U.S. Navy SEAL*

TO AN ENTREPRENEUR, *DOING* IS A TERM OF ART. It means starting, not quitting, and ultimately achieving some value that wasn't there before. Doing is the most valuable quantity there is. So why don't we?

One hundred people were asked at random over the course of this project whether they thought owning their own business, being their own boss, launching a new enterprise, and creating jobs for others was a desirable goal. Most said yes.

But when they were asked, "So why do you think most people with the idea or the dream don't start their own businesses?," 100 out of 100 answered with a one-word sentence that starts with an F. They all said, "Fear."[1]

"They know what they're talking about," said Dr. David Ouahnouna, an Israeli human performance scientist. "When a person has something important that they wish to do, they want to do, or need to do—and they are not doing it—*then some type of fear is stopping them.* Whether they admit or even realize it, a small but insistent voice is saying to them, 'I can't, I'm not strong enough, I don't have the power, I can see what's going to happen, I don't believe I can, and I don't like how this feels.' Underneath their anxiety, the person is feeling elements of more specific phobias or primary instincts like fear of the unknown, fear of loss, fear of social isolation or public humiliation, all of which trace back to the mother of all fears, fear of death."

But since the average person is not a neuroscientist, that single word *fear* covers it all—and it accounts for the resulting lost possibilities, inaction, noncommitment, nonexploration, and nonstarting for millions of people.

Yet as you'll see, fear has both a major upside and a big emotional counterpart that can tame it. Turning these emotions to your advantage is the whole purpose of the discipline we call *emotional mechanics*.

As an entrepreneur, knowing the business mechanics—the technical, operational, and financial mechanics—gets you on the field.

But you win with the emotional mechanics.

Understanding and mastering the emotional mechanics makes you UnStoppable.

---

[1] Actually, we should make it 101 because Henry Ford, one of the greatest entrepreneurs, agreed and wrote famously about fear. Ford believed that fear permeates the decision to go forward in any business. But he thought that once fear was recognized, it could be deconstructed, reappraised, and made into a positive. It seems that Ford was ahead of his time in emotional mechanics, just as he was in the other kind of mechanics.

WHAT IS EMOTIONAL MECHANICS?

The ultimate motivational force in any activity is not physical, intellectual, or technical—it is an emotional force. It's driven by just two four-letter words: *fear*—nature's great stopper, distorter, and diminisher—and another word. I was told this word repeatedly by the toughest, bravest, most UnStoppable achievers this planet has ever known: Navy SEALs, members of elite Israeli commando units, and the people who train them. And it's backed up by the experience of building a company with a multibillion-dollar market cap from scratch with a culture that is still entrepreneurial 12 years later after growing to more than 5,000 employees worldwide.

That other word that drives the emotional force is *love*. Love—as in love of teammates, love of company, love of mission, love of commanders and soldiers, love of being needed by people you admire and care about. That kind of love. You can search high and low but there is no substitute for this word, even though traditionally it's not been a word deemed appropriate for business. Yet the proof is all around us. In the sacrifices that teammates on a mission, soldiers, parents, and even strangers make for others at the risk of pain and mortal injury, the evidence says that *love is stronger than death*. So, like elite special forces instructors, we're going to use the word, too.

When both fear and love are harnessed and brought together in you, your team, and your organization, the force that results is *belief*—a force that trumps any idea, business plan, or graduate degree. No one escapes the influence of fear, love, and belief. When you understand how they're applied, you gain an extraordinary advantage for your enterprise—one that's impossible to over-value in today's hyper-competitive world.

Emotional mechanics—the ability to bring together fear and love to create belief—enables us to start, do, and succeed regardless of odds or resources.

A SEAL or an Israeli Special Forces member will tell you that when it's all on the line, how you handle emotional mechanics is the difference between mission won or lost, life and death. As an entrepreneur, there will be times when you'll be putting it all on the line, too. The stakes will be high. That's what makes emotional mechanics so important.

EXAMPLES ALL AROUND US

Star athletes tell us all the time that, at the top level, every player has the technical ability. Everyone on the tour has the ground strokes, has played thousands of games, and is in peak condition.

But the language we use to describe the difference between winners and losers on a given day is almost never about the physical. Rather, we talk about an emotional state of mind: "She just wanted it more." "He didn't get rattled." "She dug deeper than the pain." "They just know how to win." "They kept their concentration." "They have no quit." "They play as one." "She can ski right on the edge but never go over."

Herein lies that last 1 to 3 percent, a great player's winning margin.

Ask the world's highest-paid athlete, Tiger Woods. He was hailed as the second coming within months of going pro, became the world's number one golfer and stayed number one for the next 11 years. Tiger wasn't just UnStoppable, he was invincible, and the world wanted to go along for the ride.

And then, as most people know, it was suddenly over. The sex scandal. The canceled sponsors. The public ridicule. Tiger apologized on TV, quit the tour, and entered celebrity rehab.

Finally, after several months in exile, he decided to come back. There wasn't anything physically different about Tiger. The perfect mechanics of his swing and 25 years of muscle memory hadn't changed. He stepped back onto the course as always . . . but for the first time in his life, Tiger Woods couldn't win.

What *had* changed, and what he had lost, was his emotional mechanics. Tiger's legendary grip on his own confidence, pride, and concentration was being challenged by doubt, distraction, and the pressure not to fail—fear, in other words. He dropped to 58th in the rankings. He looked finished.

That's a good thing, since fear is absolutely universal.

Eric Greitens, a champion boxer, Oxford Rhodes Scholar, and officer in the Navy SEALs, wrote about the reality he found at SEAL basic training (known as BUD/S) in his book, *The Heart and the Fist:* "These were athletes: high school and college football players, water polo players, state champion wrestlers. Many of them could ace the runs, but as we'd learn over and over again in BUD/S, physical fitness mattered little without the mental fortitude to deal with fear."[3]

You may not think of yourself as a fearful person. You may not think that the great risk-taking entrepreneurs and warriors ever bask in fear. But here's why the PhDs in fear would beg to differ.

Fear is the original animal emotion—and every one of us is an active carrier. No one escapes its influence on our lives, relationships, choices, and decisions. Any successful entrepreneur who tells you he hasn't been scared or even terrified at some point in the life of his business is either lying or in a state of denial. Every seasoned warrior, every experienced actor about to take the stage, and every great athlete who ever set foot in the arena knows it, too.

So we can't take fear out of the equation. But we can learn to outwit the beast, to repurpose it and reap the benefits of doing so. Understanding a little about the brain's fear system can show us tactics for taming it.

FEAR AND THE BRAIN

As every animal knows, fear feels bad:[4] physically because of the jolt of the stress response, and mentally because of a control center in our brains that governs fear, anger, and our memories around fear. It's the notorious, walnut-sized amygdala.

[3] Eric Greitens, *The Heart and the Fist: The Education of a Humanitarian, the Making of a Navy SEAL* (Boston: Houghton Mifflin Harcourt, 2011).
[4] Berns, *Iconoclast*.

The fear response causes a whole-body stress condition that prepares us instantly for flight or fight. It dilates our pupils, raises our blood pressure, narrows our field of vision, sharpens all five senses, dries out our mouths, and covers us with sweat. The response is so automatic, these changes start before our conscious minds even pick up the scent.

Fear needs to feel bad so it can get our attention in time and make us want to avoid any situation that triggers it. That's good for the amygdala, which is programmed like the Terminator—to shoot first and ask questions later. The amygdala's job is to detect fear, rate it, remember it, and make us dodge or extinguish it . . . and like the Terminator, it is very, very good at what it does.

For the first million years of human existence, the amygdala was probably right 99 percent of the time. But today that hard-wired programming poses a big problem, because now we know something else: fear also accompanies opportunity, adventure, ground-breaking innovation, and our most worthwhile dreams of accomplishment—all key aspects of entrepreneurship. The primitive, irrational, and remorseless amygdala would stop us in our tracks if it could.

FEAR'S ACHILLES' HEEL

Luckily for you—and our economic future—the amygdala's rigid, irrational qualities are also its undoing. We can use a far more evolved, intelligent part of the brain to literally outsmart and tame the amygdala like the clumsy, primeval slug that it is. In fact, every time we step forward to take a worthwhile risk to achieve something, that's exactly what we are doing.

We are rescued from our ancient response by a part of the brain called the prefrontal cortex. And the best news of all is that we can actively condition the cortex and become quite skilled at throwing the amygdala off track. The cortex does this by *reframing*— that is, redefining and redirecting—those fear impulses. It works especially well on the three main intangible or achievement fears that, more than any others, stop us from reaching for higher accomplishments:[5]

1. fear of the unknown,
2. fear of failure and loss, and
3. fear of humiliation and social isolation.

Neuroscientists seem to agree that these are the holy trinity, the three big fears that conspire to stop us from leaving the safety of the corral and daring to deal with risk.

Programming the cortex to counter them is one of the keys to mastering emotional mechanics. We can learn to change our relationship with our fears by understanding them, seeing them, touching them, and feeling the power we unleash in ourselves each time with overcome them. And changing our relationship with our fears changes how we manage fear's three unwelcome cousins—risk, failure, and obstacles.

THE POWER OF RISK

When a retired business executive was asked late in life if there was any one thing he regretted, the man replied, "I would have ended up eighty-five anyway. I wish I had taken more risk."

In simplest terms, risk is the possibility that we might lose, with consequences. Based on what we've just discussed about fear, that's all it takes to drive the amygdala nuts and make it do everything in its power to attach fear to any kind of risk and prevent us from taking it. And since fear feels bad, risk feels bad. The problem is, we can't achieve any human progress without risk.

As a sage insurance executive I know once said, "We sail our boats every day on a sea of risk. We can't get to our destination without

---

[5] Tangible, physical fears like fear of injury, sickness, and physical pain can inhibit us in specific instances, too, but the three achievement fears are intangible and have the broadest impact on our main subjects: entrepreneuring and innovation.

navigating through it." The same applies to all of us. Bottom line: risk doesn't go with the territory, it *is* the territory—that is, if we plan to build, create, innovate, experience, achieve, or win at anything.

In our new, dynamic world, where change is accelerating all around us, the safety we feel by hiding behind a rock instead of putting ourselves in motion has become an illusion—the riskiest decision of all. As the SEALs like to say, it's always less risky to *do it* than to have it *done* to you. In live combat—the most dynamic situation there is—the deadliest action you can take is to stay in one place over time. So not moving is not an option. In the same way, as entrepreneurs, we have to change just to stay the same, just to hold onto what we've got, let alone get ahead, and the trend is going in only one direction. Change means choices, and choices mean risk.

But don't worry if you're not a risk lover.

You'll never have to be. Nearly all entrepreneurs and achievers are the opposite—they're dream, idea, and mission lovers. They accept that risk (and the fear that comes with it) is a natural condition of going somewhere—and they want to eliminate their chances of not getting there. So they become risk reducers and risk mitigators above all.

How do you minimize risk? Exactly the same way the SEALs and IDF do:

1. Get proficient on the basics *fast*, practice until they're automatic, then find some tactical advantage. Your winning ratio is always 20 percent preparing, 80 percent doing.

2. Eliminate your known disadvantages—the pitfalls, hazards, mistakes, and traps you can fix in advance.

3. Multiply your power by building a true team—a huge UnStoppable advantage.

4. Practice steering your fear—transferring it into energy to prevent it from stopping you, distorting your thinking, and ruining your timing. You must be ready to pull the switch whenever the moment of opportunity arrives, and only practice can make this possible.

Consider this example: The average skydiver wants to live as long as you do. She hates the way fear feels. But flying through the sky is what she yearns for because to her, it's life-affirming, almost spiritual. So she minimizes her risk just as the SEALs or any good entrepreneur would do: she eliminates the preventable hazards, she doesn't pull low (that is, wait too long before opening her chute), she doesn't fly without an automatic activation device, she doesn't fly under the influence, and she doesn't make high-speed landings. She practices her technicals (basic proficiency skills) and flight-checks her equipment. The result? She's got the odds of an accident down to 1 out of 300,000 on every jump, safer than driving her car to the drop zone. She reminds herself of this fact when her amygdala sends her the fear demons.

Becoming a confident, expert sailor on the sea of risk gives you a winner's edge no matter what course you take in life.

THE POWER OF FAILURE

"Failure is feedback. And feedback is the breakfast of champions."
—A fortune cookie

James Dyson invented the world's first bagless vacuum cleaner, even after every vacuum cleaner maker in the world told him for years that he shouldn't, they couldn't, and buyers wouldn't. It took him five years of tinkering in his cellar, but after 5,000 failed tries (or "prototypes," as engineers call them), he built a working model and got it to market. Within 18 months, it was the number one–selling vacuum cleaner. Now Dyson is a billionaire.

Dyson says, "I'm particularly adept at making mistakes—it's a necessity as an engineer. Each iteration of the vacuum came about because of a mistake I needed to fix. What's important is that I didn't stop at the first failure, the 50th, or the 5,000th. I never will. Believing that big companies would choose good technology—progress—over short-term profit was a big mistake. I love mistakes."[6]

---

[6] James Dyson, "My Favorite Mistake," *Newsweek*, May 29, 2011, http://www.thedailybeast .com/newsweek/2011/05/29/my-favorite-mistake-james-dyson.html.

Without exaggeration, it is *impossible* to succeed without failing your way there. Failure means learning. Failure means adjusting and fixing. Failure means measuring your limits. Failure means peeling away the outside to get to the essence. Failing means eliminating the obstacles that block your progress. Failure means getting better and stronger. For all these reasons, failure is always temporary—unless you quit.

As Thomas Edison said, you must "fail your way to success." Edison tested countless fibers over three years until he finally found the right material (a kind of carbonized bamboo) to serve as the filament for his incandescent light bulb—which changed the world. When asked about his innumerable failures, Edison replied, "I didn't fail 1,000 times, I found 1,000 ways not to make a light bulb."

No one expects you to enjoy failure, and you certainly don't want you to aim for failure. We want you to understand it and reframe it so fear of failure won't keep you from risk. Repositioning failure in our minds is one of the easier tasks in emotional mechanics, because it's an intellectual proposition. Fear of failure is powered by our instinctual fear of loss and humiliation that we consciously imagine, which prevents us from taking risks. But we can extinguish this fear when we rationally decide that failure is actually something positive—as long as it serves the mission and as long as we pick up and keep going when it happens.

SEALs use failure as a primary training tool. "We fail in little ways a thousand times a day," one SEAL said. In early training exercises, or *evolutions* as SEALs call them, the instructors often set goals that they know the students cannot reach to teach them certain functional boundaries. The overall goal is to have them experience the power of coming back—to realize their capacity not to quit until the mission succeeds.

In their book *Start-up Nation*, Dan Senor and Saul Singer say the Israeli military puts so much stock in extracting learning through failure that they conduct elaborate analysis and debriefing rituals. They rate leaders on their talent and effectiveness at debriefing their subordinates, because they consider it as crucial as any other leadership skill. It's made clear to everyone that so-called constructive or intelligent failure is acceptable as long as it's in service of improvement and ultimate mission success.

The Israelis' deep-rooted cultural attitude toward failure is seen as a key factor in that tiny nation's remarkable start-up volume, out of proportion to its size. In Israel, if you haven't tried and failed to start a business two or three times, people wonder what's the matter with you. You must be a slacker or something![7]

No team or organization will be able to compete in the dynamic new world unless they see constructive failure as a critical tool of innovation, not to be wasted. Unless it's possible to dare and fail and dare again, no organization will risk innovative thinking or get the benefit of its people's entrepreneurial power. They will be left in the dust by the organizations that do. Failure is a series of stepping stones, a strengthener, a "smartener," an irremovable part of the *doing* process. It's not supposed to be fun or painless—but if you keep at it with doggedness and intelligence, it will train you for success.

THE POWER OF OBSTACLES

Imagine the 100-yard dash at the Olympics. Ten sprinters are lined up with straight lanes in front of them to the finish line. But what if, a minute before the race, the officials put three-foot-tall hurdles on the track and said, "We have some new rules. You all have to jump these hurdles as you race." The sprinters would have a fit. "It's impossible, we're not trained, we'll get injured, we *can't*," they'd shout, and storm out in protest.

Now, just to keep things going, the officials decide to leave the hurdles up and call out the hurdlers. Ready, set, BANG! They'd be off at the gun and run as gracefully as gazelles over all the hurdles. One or two might set records and earn tickets to Disney World.

For the hurdlers, the challenge of leaping over three-foot-tall obstacles is completely normal. They do thousands of hurdles a

---

[7]Dan Senor and Saul Singer, *Start-up Nation: The Story of Israel's Economic Miracle* (New York: Twelve, 2009).

week until it becomes a key proficiency. Each new hurdle doesn't make them happier; if they drop their focus, the hurdle will still drop them. But jumping hurdles doesn't hold up their progress or sap their confidence. *They've made handling obstacles a habit.*

In much the same way, UnStoppable people accept that entrepreneuring, innovating, or embarking on any great mission is an obstacle course. It's a path lined with problems needing to be solved. But they accept this as normal. More than that, they know that they're refining their expert intuition with every hurdle they face. That means they see patterns and solutions that others don't see, often because their unconscious recognizes something familiar.[8] They stay clear headed, continue to believe that a solution exists, and keep trying until they find it. Overcoming obstacles has become a habit.

This insight is crucial for Charley Housen, the unlikely entrepreneur who built the Erving Paper Mills company and who is the actual reason why Wendy's napkins around the world are yellow. He uses this approach when presented with the glitches and problems of building his business each day. To Housen, a setback that might thwart the average business person is just another normal hurdle.

Housen learned to think this way when his uncle, the head of the family business, suddenly died. Charley was forced to leave law school and take charge of the company. The more problems and snafus he had to solve, the easier it got to grab opportunities and flip the go-switch when they appeared. Charley eventually realized that no opportunity comes free of obstacles, and there are always solutions because he'd seen so many. By doing it so often, he found he had a knack for it.

One day Charley was offered an irresistible deal—the chance to buy a warehouse full of used telephone books in rural Massachusetts for a bargain price. (And yes—four million phone books can be classified as irresistible when you're in the paper recycling business, like Charley was.) There was just one problem. The four million books were the Yellow Pages, and it would be impossible to spend the money to get all the yellow dye out of the paper and still make a

---

[8]Daniel Kahneman, *Thinking Fast and Slow.*

profit. The market for canary yellow recycled paper is rather limited, but Charley's experience told him he could deal with this obstacle. He bought the books.

It may have been luck or coincidence, but it turned out that Charley Housen had gotten friendly with Dave Thomas of Columbus, Ohio, through a business connection. He knew Dave was an entrepreneur who was starting a hamburger chain, so Charley did the natural entrepreneurial thing—the secret of success for centuries—and picked up the phone to call him. Dave needed a napkin supplier, and Charley convinced him that yellow napkins would make a lovely, distinctive accessory that would become a brand signature the world round. Also, that the yellow dye looked especially great with mustard. Charley's irresistible deal on the Yellow Pages became another entrepreneur's irresistible deal on napkins.

What to do with four million Yellow Pages' worth of scrap paper from which the dye won't come out? Just another hurdle, just another opportunity.

For a master of emotional mechanics, the formula is simple. Problems are obstacles; obstacles are temporary failures; failure poses risk; and risk inspires fear, which, when we handle it intelligently, empowers us to find solutions. That's why *obstacle* is really just another word for *opportunity*.

THE LOVE ADVANTAGE

Love has a branding problem. (Other than that, it's perfect.) For mainstream thinkers, love lives in the category generally reserved for chick flicks. It has no place in the analytical world of objectivity that good business demands.

Yet businesses are 100 percent built by, staffed by, and beholden to human beings, and if Madison Avenue can say that "America Runs on Dunkin'," we can say that human beings run on love. It is the one *free* substance that everyone wants more of, especially in the place where we spend half of our waking lives: the workplace.

But let's be clear: love comes in a variety of forms, and emotional mechanics is not advocating romantic love and affection in your place of business. It means love in the forms of belonging, respect, peer bonding, and inspiring missions that you undertake with others.

In businesses and even in the military, when the positive emotional factor of love is allowed to function anywhere near its true capacity, it produces a remarkable cause and effect. It unleashes confidence, innovation, creativity, and emotional investment. It is said that a person will give you his back and his brawn for a paycheck, but he'll give his heart and his brains for love—and will sacrifice to keep it.

Dan Brodsky-Chenfeld, a world champion team skydiver, told me about this form of power, especially in true teams. Teammates love two things even more than themselves and their own preservation: belonging to a group of teammates whom they admire and respect enough to trust with their lives, and having such a group need and believe in them. They will go to great lengths—suffering pain, misery, and discomfort without quitting, even making the ultimate sacrifice—not to lose the team's admiration or let it down.

Bottom line: This kind of love adds up to humanity's number one unlimited, clean alternative energy source—*the only force strong enough to tame fear* with all its attendant demons when it is properly deployed. Wouldn't it make the simplest common sense to tap this free force in any type of business—not just entrepreneurial start-ups—to boost energy, loyalty, positive attitude, and competiveness?

Graham Weston will tell you that, of all the factors that enabled Rackspace to grow from 4 employees to 5,000 and to rise above dozens of competitors, love is the most powerful. He's referring to several kinds of love: love of their shared mission (to deliver Fanatical Support), love of their customers, love of their common values and their crazy traditions, and the love that unites teammates who are striving to accomplish something great together. "We'd all do anything to keep this feeling that we get at work alive," Graham says. "Succeeding is how we hang on to it."

THE UNSURPASSED POWER OF BELIEF

There's one all-purpose tool that's more valuable than any other one in the box—one that trumps any kind of natural-born talent. And while philosophers and theologians have debated its definition for eons, we won't. When Henry Ford said simply, "If you think you can or think you can't, you're right," he didn't mean a spiritual abstraction, he meant that belief is a real, self-fulfilling prophesy. This is the inner voice that "talks us into it," that thrills us with desire because we see our dream as possible for us to achieve. Thinking "it's possible" triggers confidence, determination, and energy. Thinking the opposite makes any task impossible.

Belief is a mental and physical, conscious and unconscious condition, the only combined force strong enough to knock down the wall of Fear, Uncertainty, and Doubt (FUD)—the master stopper of the universe.

Being in a state of belief literally manufactures the success factors for us: it creates a clearer vision of our objective, decriminalizes risk, boosts our pain tolerance, motivates us to inspire others, and feeds the fire of hope. Belief gives us the power to persevere beyond where we ever thought we could, and solve what couldn't be solved.

Without belief, our thoughts act against us ruthlessly, wielding FUD to make the emotional and psychological barrier a wall we can't climb.

The outcome of mastering emotional mechanics is belief. Ultimately, in an organization of any size, only a Belief Culture can sustain and unleash entrepreneurship, initiative, innovation, and joy. Unfortunately, all too many companies operate instead with Fear Cultures, which inevitably kill the entrepreneurial spirit.

For this reason, Fear Cultures will be unable to compete in the new economic order of the twenty-first century.

- Emotional mechanics translates love and fear into belief—the ultimate motivating forces.

- Your ability to believe correlates with your ability to succeed.

- Fear is natural. Everybody has it. You can choose to turn it into power. The greatest performers know this truth: fear is your friend.

- If there is something you want to do but you're not doing it, some kind of fear, conscious or unconscious, is holding you back.

- You need to see, touch, and experience your own fear, even once, to start steering it.

- Handling fear directly impacts how you handle its cousins: risk, failure, and obstacles.

- The most powerful teams and best organizations run on love and belief.

4

How to Master Emotional Mechanics Like the Experts

It's okay to have butterflies. You just have to get them to fly in formation.

—Melissa Lukin, Outward Bound

LIKE ALMOST EVERY OTHER ABLE-BODIED Israeli citizen, performance expert and psychologist Dr. David Ouahnouna has spent time in the army. He also happens to be an expert in Krav Maga, the unique Israeli method of self-defense training. He told us the story of what happened the day after a terrorist got over the fence near his village and stabbed a yeshiva student, not far from his house. Yeshiva students are members of an Orthodox Jewish sect that studies ancient Hebrew texts for hours a day. Pretty much the opposite of a football lineman on a Texas high school team. The whole neighborhood was almost paralyzed with fear after the attack. Parents wanted to keep their kids inside, and the kids felt depressed, violated, and vulnerable.

Dr. Ouahnouna went down to the school the next day, got the kids together, and gave them a special course in Krav Maga. "After a couple of days, there was this transformation in these kids," he said. "The kids were walking around with their chests out, heads high, ready to jump in and defend their friends if it ever happened again. They didn't really know any Krav Maga, only one or two moves I taught them. But the difference was, they now *believed*. They knew what to do, they knew they'd always have a chance. They said, 'It's possible for me.' All they did was switch their thinking from victim to defender. It was amazing to see."

Making emotional mechanics work for you is as fundamentally simple as what Dr. Ouahnouna did. It involves just a little bit of mental magic, a few rules of thumb, and repetition in real conditions so that as soon as possible, you can function, improve, and enable yourself or your team to believe. The central UnStoppable theme is to learn the essence in a short time, then start doing and practicing it for a long time. It's the same process for fear training or anything else.

TRUE TEAM: THE NUMBER ONE FEAR TAMER

Navy SEALs are some of the most extraordinary individuals on the planet. Yet once they make it through the most rigorous training in the world, you will never hear them talk about themselves as individual SEALs; they only talk in terms of team: "He was a team guy." Or "When I joined the teams . . ." Or "I've been with the teams for 18 years."

This is because SEALs know that nobody ever does it alone. And as great as any individual's power might be, it goes up exponentially in the mutual support structure and creative circuitry that exists in a small team. The elite of the elite consider this the *ultimate multiplier* of motivation and the ability to tolerate and manage risk, discomfort, and fear.

Teams spread out the fear and share its burden, which automatically helps to control it. They are a kind of love power plant, generating the kind of love that overwhelms and tames fear.

But not fake teams. Not the clichéd kind that corporate speakers prattle on about. A true team is an entirely different organism: a fusion of individuals into one working being. Members of true teams need one another to succeed, and they all know it. Thus there is no advantage to doing anything but building each other up. They get scared together, fail together, struggle together, overcome obstacles together, and win together. Because of the love and trust that develops, they will put themselves at risk, suffer, and sacrifice for one another to a degree they would never do for themselves. A true team is an UnStoppable team—a secret weapon that can maximize anyone's ability to achieve.

Chances are that as you're sitting here reading this, you're not yet a member of any such team. But don't worry—no one is born into an entrepreneurial team. Every founding member starts by himself or herself, as an individual with a dream. Destined teammates who are "casting the net" in search of one another will find each other in time.

We'll leave this concept here for now, except to say that it's so elemental, it changes the entrepreneur's eternal question. Most people believe that the entrepreneur should ask from day one, like a mantra, "What's my idea?"

But the UnStoppable version of the entrepreneurial question has two parts, the order of which is unimportant: "What's my idea? Who's my team?" Both parts are equally essential.

THE MENTAL MAGIC OF REFRAMING

Given the immense power allotted to the fear center in the brain—led by the amygdala and its neural and hormonal support systems—it's a wonder that we can trick and bypass the whole thing using a simple, conscious technique formulated in a recently evolved part of our brains, just behind our foreheads. But we can. As we discussed in Chapter 3, the most common way it's done is by conditioning the prefrontal cortex to redefine and redirect the fear impulses.

This kind of strategy is what neuroscientists call *cognitive reappraisal*, a conscious, proactive shift by the cortex that says, "You know that thing you thought you knew? It's really something else—something better." Advertising agencies used to use these thought shifters every day.[1] They called it *positioning* a brand. For example: Pork isn't a salty, fatty meat that clogs the arteries, it's really "the other white meat," and we all know white meat's good for you. Don't worry about getting chapped hands when you do dishes; Palmolive Liquid is really hand softener in disguise. Guinness isn't beer; it's nourishing food. It all comes down to a simple message: you thought this was less, but it's really more.

The best term for this is *reframing:* taking an idea out of one context or frame and sticking it into another that casts it in a completely different and usually better light.

When reframing is done right, it changes perception instantaneously and permanently, extinguishing our notions and thus changing emotions. Reframing is one of our universal tools. For example, it will be our most vital Accelerated Proficiency tool when we discuss branding and differentiating for any business later on. Reframing is also a power tool in selling. Even irrational impulses can be overruled by this conscious, rational tool—especially fear.

Here's a dramatic story I heard from a friend about how he cured his lifelong fear of flying in a single day. He did it with one momentous reframing thought. Whenever he got on a plane, his imagination ran wild. Every new bump or sound was *it*—just what the doomed passengers on flight so-and-so must've heard before the wing fell off. He knew he was suffering from a full-blown phobia, but he couldn't shake it. Then by chance, this guy's girlfriend got a job as a flight attendant and started flying dozens of places a week. He knew she flew with great pilots on safe planes. He never worried for a minute when she was flying because he knew she'd come back safely.

And then one day his girlfriend showed up with a pair of plane tickets. They were going to her best friend's wedding. This was non-negotiable, and a few weeks later, he found himself sitting next to

---

[1] We say "used to" because advertisers in the days of *Mad Men* were wizards at positioning, the art of the big, differentiated selling idea that could set a brand apart for decades. These days, we look at advertising and often can't even determine what product is being advertised, let alone why it's the best choice.

her on the plane, about to leave the gate. He felt the usual nauseating panic. And then he looked at her, and had this thought: "Anita is here on her airline trip, sitting in her seat like she does every day. I'm just riding along on her plane. She'll be safe and get home like always, so I'll get home too. Anita's plane is always safe and you just happen to be sitting on it with her."

In that moment his fear literally vanished. For the next three hours, his mind and body experienced the thoughts and sensations of flying without fear. The next time he flew alone, he remembered his frame and talked to himself continually before the flight: "If I just substituted Anita for me in this seat, I'd know this flight would be safe. She's sitting here instead of me. We'll get home fine, like always."

The rest of the story is that our friend soon became a Platinum-level frequent flyer enjoying hundreds of trips all over the world. Occasionally his amygdala would send him a few butterflies. But he always had his frame to tamp them back down.

Metaphors—the most powerful linguistic device used in storytelling, poetry, and song—are just ways to reframe. As we'll see, they are also a critical tool used by the best reframers to make their frames convincing and memorable. A metaphor asks you to think of something you know as something else: "Golf is a fickle lover." "Drugs are the devil." "Speed kills." "Your pain is your power." "Fifty is the new forty." Or that one James Dyson used: to an engineer, "a mistake is just a prototype." "Failure equals learning."

If you're afraid of heights, you'd think the higher you go up in a plane, the scarier it would get. But to pilots, higher is just a different frame. It's always safer and better. It gives you time to deal with emergencies and even better gas mileage when your fuel is low. So pilots live by the metaphor, "Altitude is your friend."

When you recast mistakes and failure in your own mind as James Dyson does, their sting can vanish, all because of a deliberate, conscious thought that *you* control—one that is smarter than your amygdala.

You'll get your reframes from a variety of places, including from the lessons and wisdom of teachers, coaches, and leaders. (We've already insinuated a handful into your consciousness through the pages of this book.) They'll also appear to you in the process of getting in motion, walking the road, and gathering personal expert experience. What's more, reframes happen most readily in teams because of the synergy of creativity and thought that happens there—yet another of a team's multipliers.

THE SECRET OF SELF-TALK

In the brain, conscious thought speaks to us in the words of our native language, and reframing is no exception. The logic, snap, and memorable nature of this language is critical for recall when we need it most—under stress. You pick it up from others or originate it for yourself.

Peak performers don't think it's crazy or odd to talk to themselves. They think it'd be crazy if you didn't. All performers who are operating under stress talk to themselves continually—while learning and practicing, but also when reminding themselves to execute key steps that are needed to avoid disaster, whether landing a plane, aiming a rifle, or preparing to deliver a speech before a skeptical audience.

Since time immemorial, every new sailor has been taught to navigate into a harbor with this alliterative phrase: "Red right returning." It means keep the red buoys on the right and you'll stay in the channel. Every single time you enter the channel, for the rest of your boating life, a little voice will speak to you, or you'll say out loud the three Rs.

As these examples illustrate, effective self-talk is essential for feeling in control and anticipating what comes next in high-stress situations. It lets you step aside from the most acute fear and steer the fear that's left over.

MICRO-SCRIPTS ARE THE SELF-TALK SECRET

Peak performers from jet pilots to Olympic athletes use what we call Micro-Scripts over and over—those short, easy-to-remember phrases they trust, like "Red right returning." SEALs and Israeli commanders train with them every day. For each life-saving lesson a SEAL learns, he also gets a pithy, unforgettable rule. "Tap, rack, bang" clears a jammed magazine in a gunfight. "Attack the crack" gets you into the room where a terrorist is hiding with a gun. "Suck the mud" is what you do when an enemy boat arrives overhead. "Canopy in sight, pull right" is how you yank your parachute away from a collision course.

After years of practice, you may not say these Micro-Scripts aloud, but your mind will still repeat them in a whisper. A sailor will hear "When in doubt, let it out" in his head during a big gust. And while the process of mitigating real fear can be complex, reframing it starts the same way, with a few potent words of self-talk: "Fear is my friend." "You can sleep when you're dead." "You can do it because you've done it." "This shit is what we like."

We've talked about reframing failure itself, one of the big three fears, with phrases like "Failing is learning," "You must fail your way to success," and "Every No gets me closer to Yes." We can find similar reframes for fear of humiliation, like the fear of public speaking: "Just imagine the audience is naked!"

But fear of uncertainty and the unknown—that's a horse of a different color . . .

THE SIMPLE POWER OF "KNOWING WHAT TO DO"

Fear of uncertainty and the unknown is the big bogeyman for most of us humans. Fear of the unknown has it all: death, injury, loss, terror, failure—you name it. Our brains instinctively hate "not knowing" when something is going on around us that might affect us, so they will fill in the blanks with optical illusions and (often dire) assumptions when no meaningful answer is available.

Uncertainty makes everyone nervous. It makes SEAL candidates "ring the bell" and quit during basic training as often as pain, cold, or any other tangible form of suffering.

But just knowing what's in store, knowing you know what to do because you've done it or seen it, is like a miracle cure for the fear of the unknown. Here's one remarkable example.

The epilogue, after three years of battling and throwing his clubs in the pond like the rest of us, is that Tiger has finally won another big tournament and appears to be getting back on track. If he stays there, it will be because he regained his mastery of those emotional mechanics.

UNDERSTANDING FEAR

Emotional mechanics gives you your Power Set, the third leg of the stool in Accelerated Proficiency. To master it, you need to know a little bit about fear. Here's why.

For our own survival, over the past million years Mother Nature has given us love and fear. Love is positive and proactive: love of belonging, love of country, love of ideas, love of success. But love is complex and needs time to develop and grow.

Fear does not. Fear is quick and fear is dumb. Fear is primitive and reactive, easier to wire into ancient living things in the beginning, when the number one item on their daily to-do list was to avoid being eaten. So Nature made fear the default: deep, automatic, and redundant. Fear and its unwelcome relatives (risk, obstacles, and failure) form an immediate barrier that, as neuroscientist Gregory Berns explains in his book *Iconoclast*, can literally change our perception, block our imagination, and make millions of us stop before we even start or make us quit too soon. Fear is the great limiter.[2]

But fear also has a huge human upside. Fear contains tremendous, tireless energy. Fear turned around is a major *motivating force* that humans have used to push themselves forward since time began. So fear is also the source of great power—but it only works if we don't let our fear response stop us before we start. If we learn to accept and direct it, fear provides the electricity to sharpen our edge, juice our senses, and stiffen our persistence. That means fear is also a gift and opportunity.

---

[2] Gregory Berns, *Iconoclast: A Neuroscientist Reveals How to Think Differently* (Boston: Harvard Business Review Press, 2010).

As we've seen, SEAL training is world famous for its five-day set of trials called Hell Week. Most candidates fail to get through it and are dropped from the program. They must spend five straight days and nights with no sleep under brutal conditions. They swim long distances in 50-degree water, perform endless physical training exercises, and maneuver heavy rubber boats onto sharp rocks in strong surf, without letup. There are no performance waivers or excuses. If you stop, you're instantly dropped from the program. Only those with serious injuries like broken limbs or pneumonia are allowed to "roll back" to try again with the next class.

None of the trials of Hell Week are described in advance. All the students know when the week begins is that they will be subjected to untold misery, pain, and pressure. The instructors use fear of the unknown like the Grim Reaper to induce the biggest percentage to quit the first day. They constantly tell exhausted, battered, freezing troops that what they've just suffered through is the easy warm-up. Not knowing what horrors are in store, and fearing that they're already nearing the breaking point, students quit in droves because of uncertainty and doubt.

Here's what blew me away. I talked to a SEAL who had done Hell Week *twice*.

He'd broken his leg after the first one, so he was rolled back to the incoming class. He got a second chance but had to do Hell Week all over again. He said, "The second time, I knew what the evolutions were, the instructors' tricks, and I knew I had done it. It was just as cold, wet, and physically tough. But mentally, it was easy. The hardest part the first time was just that uncertainty. Without that, it was like a piece of cake. Ninety-nine percent of this is mental."

―――

PROCEDURES AND AUTOMATICS

SEALs also deal with uncertainty using something that one called *Procedures and Automatics*. One of the best fear mitigators is the calming and confidence effect people get from simply remembering their training, mentally rehearsing rules and procedures as the pressure mounts. This is the simple effect of knowing what to do. Having these preset steps is a primary method that we all can use to avoid panic in the most stressful situations.

Imagine the fear and stress you'd feel if a loved one were suddenly injured and bleeding in front of you, evidently in the process of succumbing to anaphylactic shock. Now imagine that you had just completed an excellent first-aid course as preparation for a job as a volunteer ambulance attendant. Doesn't that feel a little different?

Peak performers know that practicing the same procedures grooves their reactions so they become automatic. The combination of repeating them consciously and internalizing them unconsciously is one of the best tools for emotional mechanics that we have. "When things get particularly hot," said one SEAL, "we can switch our brains onto our procedures. We know they work and we can work them."

———

EXTINGUISHING

Author and neuroscientist Gregory Berns uses a term he calls *extinguishing*. He claims that fear triggers can be reset in the amygdala by taking repeated action. The amygdala expects that action to produce a feared result, but it does not. The effect is to extinguish the trigger for the response. Without the trigger, the action doesn't generate the fear.

This is a big reason why entrepreneurs who are used to defeating obstacles and problems no longer automatically flinch when they encounter one. Instead, they can turn their power to attacking and solving it, because with practice, they've removed the fear triggers that distract other people. It's an enormous advantage to have.

Extinguishing is probably 90 percent due to good old-fashioned familiarity and practice, and it's one of the most basic antidotes to fear there is. It's one more reason to get in motion ASAP and start *doing* to get over the unknowns. It can be that simple once you get started.

━━━━━

FEAR TRAINING

Trainers in the Israeli Defense Force have learned that by confronting controlled situations that reproduce *real* fear under the guidance of a deeply trusted leader-instructor, students can teach themselves how to flip their own internal switches and take action without hesitation.

The instructor-psychologists said that a remarkable bonus comes to the individuals who undergo such training. The mental process they internalize is translated into other fear-inducing activities in other parts of their lives, *including their later professional lives*. Their bodies learn to adjust all the variables of feeling and sensation that are unique to each of us and that can't be scripted from the outside. Life-changing results can happen for students within six to ten days.

The big insight was that this kind of conditioning can be relevant to anyone who wants to habituate to risk and high-stress environments—including an entrepreneur.

There is much more to this story than we can cover in this book, but the Israelis make a compelling case that experiential training like this holds a key to accelerating a student's vital skills in emotional mechanics. The trainers believe it can be the basis of an amazingly effective educational paradigm.

━━━━━

FEAR ENERGY TURNED AROUND

The net result of every tactic and strategy we've discussed is *not* that the flames of fear are snuffed out—they never can be. But their destructive power is transmuted into positive energy. The same flames that could incinerate your dreams can serve instead for cooking and heating, tempering steel and forging tools. Remember, the heightened heart rate, sharpened senses, and overall edginess caused by the fear response prepare us physically for action. No one who understands performance in competitive environments would ever consider giving up that advantage—it's part of the UnStoppable edge. The solution is to block the path the amygdala wants us to take—escape, avoidance, or hiding in place—and let this energy rebound in the only direction that remains: *forward*.

GOODNESS

There's a value at the beginning and the end of all this, one too big to get a number on a list. It's not *greatness*, as in wealth or power or winning the most trophies. The word for it is *goodness*, and there's no better or simpler one. It's a different kind of measure, and we think every human being has a notion of what it is and wants it for themselves and those they love. They want it in the mission they pursue, in the companies where they work. They want to root for it and see it win in the end. They want to know it's how they got the chance they had to touch greatness.

Goodness does not make you UnStoppable in this world. But it does make more people want to support you, asking nothing in return. It makes more potentially magnificent team members want to join forces with you. It makes your customers happier, your products better, your decisions easier, and your risks smaller.

Perhaps the best thing about becoming an entrepreneur is that you get to choose exactly what part goodness will play in your life from moment one. And whether or not goodness alone can make what you do bigger, it will *always* make what you do better.

- True teams are the fastest, most dependable fear tamer. They spread risk and leverage the motivating force of love.

- Rational reframing of irrational fear will outwit the brain's fear center.

- The simplest techniques like self-talk, procedures and automatics, and extinguishing are powerful tools for handling uncertainty and unknowns.

- Motion makes you practice emotional mechanics. Practice makes it personal, and personal makes you learn.

- Studies show that fear training that habituates students to risk and performance under stress can not only be accelerated, but its effects can also extend to students' professional lives.

PART II

Getting Down to Business

Your UnStoppable Tool Kit

5

School of Everything You Need to Know (in an Hour)

There were two really big things that Graham Weston and I brought back from our worldwide journey to the find the secret of entrepreneurship. One was the essence—a deeper understanding of the true heart of entrepreneurship. The other was a fresh insight into how to package the principles of entrepreneurial success into a business tool kit that you can carry around with you, starting on day one.

The master principles presented in the chapters that follow are a distillation of hours of discussions with Graham and his partners, years of exposure to Rackspace, and the lessons received from many great mentors—business experts, successful entrepreneurs, teachers and trainers, elite warriors, and many more. They're principles that could only be articulated *after* visiting with the obsessive business builders who've made Israel into a Start-up Nation, being exposed to ideas like Accelerated Proficiency and Emotional

Mechanics, and studying the visceral wisdom of the Navy SEALs and other unique team-makers we were fortunate enough to meet.

So welcome to your first day of school. You may already have a college degree or an MBA, so you've been to other schools—but never one quite like this. This is the School of Everything You Need to Know in an Hour, otherwise known as Accelerated Proficiency U. It's built on the notion that the best businesspeople can tell you everything they know about succeeding—at least, everything they can verbalize—in about an hour. And while there's a lot of other things they know, they can't tell you about it because its nonverbal intuition, learned and absorbed through years of trying and doing. And that is the only way to get it.

When you become an entrepreneur, you'll understand that you'll never graduate from this school—and you won't want to, because entrepreneurship is a permanent process of learning above all else. Each time you make a mistake, try out an idea, open a new market, or solve a problem, you learn something. And contrary to what you might hear in business school, the most important lesson to absorb—the lesson that matters more than accounting techniques, business plan mechanics, product development strategies, or anything else—is *learning how to succeed with customers*. That non-quantitative priority sets you up to keep learning how to do it faster, better, cheaper, smarter on *their* terms, and *always* with an eye toward how to make it easier for them, starting from day one and stopping never.

As Bill Clinton once said, entrepreneurship is to "learn and keep comin'." Once-innovative companies that start falling behind are the ones that have decided to stop learning.

We won't be providing you with the technical education that you can find in basic books on accounting, finance, and the like. You're here to get the big principles using the "wax on, wax off" approach. Following these principles is what makes people UnStoppable at key times in their careers. It's the main reason Rackspace broke away from the competition and eventually took the lead in its category. Rackspace didn't invent its early technology. It wasn't the most innovative or well-financed company in the field and certainly not the most well-known. But today, most of its early competitors—which were much bigger companies at the time—are gone or have been absorbed, while Rackspace has surpassed $1 billion in revenue and is number one in its specialty around the world.

Rackspace focused on a few small things that became big things because they kept doing them—constantly getting better and better. That's all we want you to do.

Last, I may have given you the impression that I look down on aspects of academia and "air-conditioned classrooms," but you must never think I disdain education. Just the opposite. Education will be the world's savior and the gateway for new entrepreneurship, not to mention the only way America can compete with other nations that are producing thousands of university graduates every week. MBA programs are very valuable in teaching administrative, financial, and organizational skills that enable scale at big companies, helping them to coax out greater efficiencies.

The point is merely that there is a big distinction between what most academic institutions are about and what our school is about. The difference is summed up very simply: the Optimizers versus the Entrepreneurs.

THE OPTIMIZERS VERSUS THE ENTREPRENEURS

Nothing in nature exists without an opposite. The opposite of Entrepreneur is Optimizer. Teaching the Optimizer mind-set and skills is the traditional default for academic institutions, and it's the hiring basis for many traditional companies.

It's important to understand the difference. We like to periodically align ourselves by asking, "Am I acting like an Optimizer or an Entrepreneur here? Am I using Optimizer language or Entrepreneur language? Is the decision I just made what an Optimizer would do, or have I chosen the Entrepreneur's path?" We ask these kinds of questions all the time, and framing both sides just makes it clearer.

Which One Are You?

An Optimizer's job is not to encourage disruption within an organization. It's to keep the organization running smoothly, efficiently, and predictably so that it can sustain itself into the future.

- Optimizers tend to be devoted to process.
- Optimizers create and spread efficiencies.
- Optimizers often outsource their learning, drawing wisdom from outside consultants and acquired businesses.
- Optimizers focus on eliminating weaknesses in employees and in the system.
- Optimizers promote predictability and planning.
- Optimizers like to validate their ideas and strategies with lots of data.
- Optimizers tend to make decisions and pursue changes deliberately and cautiously.
- Optimizers get paid to eliminate risks.

Pay particular attention to that last bullet point. It's crucial to understanding the difference between Optimizers and Entrepreneurs. Both groups would prefer to avoid risks. But whereas Optimizers build their careers around risk-avoidance, Entrepreneurs know they don't get paid unless they take risks.

Some Entrepreneurs have a bias against people with the Optimizer mentality, but that's as foolish as believing that New York City could operate without traffic lights or a municipal code. The fact is that any successful organization—especially one that scales into a big, sophisticated operation—needs the strengths, talents and skills of both Optimizers and Entrepreneurs. Entrepreneurs get things moving; they innovate, energize, and promote change. Optimizers bring the consistency and quality control that big companies and mass markets demand.

The problem comes when Optimizers and Entrepreneurs get out of balance in a company—when management spends too much time protecting and honing its big gilded assets and not enough learning, innovating, and keeping the founders' entrepreneurial spirit alive. In our new economic era of accelerating change, companies will have to keep changing and innovating just to maintain their place in whatever market they're in. Companies that want to compete will have to keep their entrepreneurial cultures alive in deed, not just in word but in actions, and from the top on down through every level of their organizations.

THE CHALLENGE FOR ANY COMPANY

When a workplace is tipped too much to the Optimizer side, Entrepreneurial employees tend to flee. An entrepreneurial thinker doesn't always have to be the boss, but she does need the opportunity to think, make, and build, not just manage. If you try to squeeze an Entrepreneur into an Optimizer mold, you'll lose her. This isn't just a cultural problem; it's a big strategic problem for any company large or small that wants to stay competitive in the new era. We'll address the solution later.

You're hearing it now because you'll multiply your chances of success by addressing these issues starting from day one. Even if you're running a lowly start-up with three employees, start focusing *now* on how you're going to keep your entrepreneurial priorities front and center, avoid the pitfall of tilting too far toward the Optimizer side, and develop an entrepreneurial belief culture that will remain intact while you grow to three thousand and then to three hundred thousand employees.

That means growing cultures of learning, innovation, problem-solving, mission focus, true teams, and market savvy—as contrasted with a culture built around bureaucracy, conformity, and control by fear. Entrepreneurial companies are dedicated to giving people first what they want most—including their own employees. Customers want good and fair value from a trusted relationship. Employees want to be valued members of a winning team on an inspiring mission. Striving constantly to provide both is the entrepreneurial way.

OUR MISSION AT ACCELERATED PROFICIENCY U.

Our charter is to teach you the most essential principles of a few core subjects in about an hour each. This will allow you to put yourself in motion and start the process of teaching yourself through hands-on experience as soon as possible. Self-teaching is the highest-yield learning method because it's custom-fit to your learning style, your strengths, your prior experiences, your immediate challenges, your everything. Physical experience is the mother of emotional mechanics and of learning that stays vibrant over time.

However, teaching yourself does not mean doing it alone. You'll always receive help from mentors, coaches, and partners. Teaching yourself just means not expecting others to give you the answers because, well, they don't have *the* answers. They have *their* answers . . . which may not be yours.

You find your answers only by being in motion in the real world—by filtering your experiences through your own background and personality.

Finally, as we've noted, the Accelerated Proficiency method is built around a Skill Set, a Rules Set, and a Power Set. The skills and rules are three or four fundamentals or rules of thumb—heuristics—that will boost your chances of success while helping you avoid traps and pitfalls. Remember the boat captain who still repeats "red right returning" to himself the 10,000th time he approaches the channel.

Your Power Set begins with your first fearful step into the physical reality—the skydiver's first step out of a perfectly good airplane, the moment when a rodeo rider first lowers his butt onto the spine of a bull, or the morning when you tell your boss—or maybe even your mom—that you're quitting your familiar job and joining the start-up full time. It's the moment you switch from mentally doing to physically doing—from lying on the shore to getting wet in the water. After that, it's about repetition and the ingrained learning that comes with it.

That's what you have to look forward to. Thank you for coming to orientation. Starting in the next chapter, we'll cover exactly what new or even experienced entrepreneurs need to know about ideas, strategies, teams, customers, products, getting famous, and more—each in about an hour.

- The best businesspeople can tell you everything they know about succeeding in about an hour. However, this is just the wisdom they can verbalize. The rest, they can't; it's expert intuition that they don't know how they know, that they've developed from years of doing. You'll get it too by heeding their advice, then doing these things yourself.
- The opposite of the Entrepreneurs are the Optimizers. Both are important to a company's success. But we need to frame both sides to know the differences between them.
- The Entrepreneur's rallying cry is "Learn, Baby, Learn!" Companies that stop inspiring and innovating have decided to stop learning.
- As an entrepreneur, your number one job on day one is not technical; it's figuring out how to succeed with customers.
- The Skills Set and Rules Set in Accelerated Proficiency are technical and simple to convey. The Power Set is emotional, time-intensive, and can't be simulated in school.
- However, your Power Set can be greatly enhanced via Accelerated Proficiency when you trigger—then overcome—real emotions in training. In this way, emotional mechanics are transferrable.
- Optimizer versus Entrepreneur: Which one are you?

6

The Big Picture in an Hour
Ideas, People, and Execution

IDEAS, PEOPLE, AND EXECUTION are the three words at the heart of every successful enterprise. They won't tell you exactly what tactics you're going to focus on each day; that comes next. But they'll frame up the big picture of what your mission is about. The big picture aligns the little picture—the individual decisions and actions that move you forward, one step at a time. Any Navy SEAL will tell you that you need a constant, seamless scan between big picture and little picture. Big picture/little picture. The Israeli Defense Force experts consider their constant habit of calibrating big picture/little picture to be one of their key success factors. They require every member of a true team to internalize it, too, in order for them to reach their highest battlefield potential. So we're going to spend a moment here on the big picture.

When I boil it down from everything I've read and studied, I think most experts would agree that every aspect of business can be extrapolated from these three general categories:

- *Idea* is the what and why. That means it covers mission, vision, value proposition, nature of product and service, innovation, differentiation, problem and solution, and so forth.
- *People* is the who and the human. It covers the founders, managers, teams, culture, talent, integrity, energy, and commitment on the inside, as well as relationships with customers, vendors, and partners on the outside.
- *Execution* is the how, where, and when. It means bringing the idea to life via performance, features, production, marketing, sales, supply chain, strategic planning, and customer service.

The questions that are debated endlessly are, "In what order should we tackle these three key elements? And which is most important?" The answers are, "All at once" and "All of the above." They are completely interdependent, each worthless without the others.

Yet their qualities are separate and the weight you give each one varies at different stages of the business. Most people rank them in this order for entrepreneurs starting a business: Idea, then People, then Execution. I disagree. So listen up, because we're going to have a reality check on all three.

EVERYTHING YOU NEED TO KNOW ABOUT IDEAS

The Perfect One

To start a business, you need one of those can't-miss, million-dollar ideas like the hula hoop—an idea that you can prototype in your basement, then show to a *Fortune 500* company that will snap it up, guaranteed. Just don't forget to make the 43 people you've told about it swear on their lives to keep it secret, and make investors sign a 12-page nondisclosure agreement so the idea stealers don't cop it and get that guaranteed $100 million for themselves because your idea is that good.

You know it's true because you learned it in school: "There is nothing more powerful than an idea whose time has come." "Build a better mousetrap and the world will beat a path to your door."

In your dreams.

Here's the reality, in the words of author and entrepreneur Tim Ferriss, as quoted in *Do More Faster: TechStars Lessons to Accelerate Your Startup* (a really good book by the founders of start-up incubator TechStars, David Cohen and Brad Feld—folks who get pitched hundreds of fail-safe ideas a month): "Trust me, your idea is worthless."

And speaking of mousetraps, you know what people *really* think when you show them a better one, one that will require them to trash all their old mousetraps that work fine, train their overworked employees how to use your new-fangled gadget, and put them at risk of getting fired when your supposedly brilliant innovation doesn't work (and the premises are suddenly aswarm with hungry, squealing rodents)?

People think you are a pain in the ass.

The key to launching a great business is *not* a brilliant idea, nor is it a brand-new, solar-powered, digitally-controlled mousetrap. You do not need to start with a perfect, fully-formed, fail-safe, once-in-a-lifetime idea to eventually succeed and become a millionaire in business. Likewise, you don't need to go around being paranoid, protecting the idea you have from grave robbers and thieves who lurk in every investor's doorway. Here's why.

People Don't Pay Money for Ideas

The reason your idea is worthless, according to *Do More Faster*, is that except in the movies, there is no market for ideas about new products and services that currently exist solely in your head. No one pays for ideas because they are a dime a dozen. Everyone has them in proportion to the number of beers they've consumed after work. Also, you can be sure that, whatever your new idea may be, someone, somewhere is already working on their own version of it.

People pay for *ideas that have been executed:* ideas that have been turned into real, working prototypes and start-up enterprises through the skills, determination, soul, and grit of an entrepreneur. The ones that have been executed are those that someone believed in enough to put everything on the line for, making mistakes and fixing them until a problem was solved, because they wanted to hold their dream in their hands. They wanted to prove the naysayers wrong.

Investors—at least not professional investors—don't invest in ideas either. They invest in the human vessel that harbors those ideas and *will execute on them.* This is not a cliché; venture capitalists, private equity masters, and others with money to invest really do bet primarily on what they believe is the fire, the enthusiasm, the resilience, and the resourcefulness of you and your people, because they know this next timeless truth about ideas . . .

All Ideas Change, Even Great Ones

The reason your idea is worthless—at least in its current form, before you've built it—is because it will change anyway, often radically, between what's in your business plan and what you eventually learn will work with customers.

This is a law unto itself. *Your idea will change.* Your business will be different six months or a year from now than when you started. An informal poll of people who run start-up incubator firms and see dozens and dozens of founders starting companies every year shows that 40 to 50 percent of those who come to them make a major pivot in the first few months. They often eject their original genius idea completely in favor of a more opportune one, because once they get into motion and test assumptions in real markets, they bump into the true opportunity, lying behind a doorway they hadn't seen.

This is a crucial big picture/little picture principle. If you're willing to adapt to reality when you see it—not give up or quit, but adjust your priorities and change your idea to meet the real demand that the market and customers show you—you will find your success. When you keep your sense of the big picture—your true mission—you'll be able to adjust the little picture as needed. Don't confuse that with giving up, because it's something very different; it's finding the clearer path. And that usually means changing, or at least tweaking, your big idea.

Rackspace became a wildly successful managed hosting company, renting out computing space on servers it sets up and maintains. But it didn't start out that way. In fact, the term *managed hosting* hadn't even been coined yet when Rackspace was started in the late nineties. The business was IT services—more accurately, three San Antonio college friends who hired themselves out to wire computer networks for local businesses to make some extra money. While performing those gigs, they got a chance to talk and listen to a variety of customers. And the team happened upon a simple, unfilled need: businesses needed more computing capacity, but didn't always have the resources or the volume to hire IT staff and build a data center. Customers started asking whether they could help them solve this problem. They realized that if they set up and maintained a rack of servers and just rented customers the amount of computing they needed, they'd pay for the service.

The rest is Rackspace history.

Great News

Do not get discouraged by this plain truth about ideas—that there's no magic bullet. It is actually the best news you could hear because it means that an idea's entrepreneurial value is shaped in your hands. It's under your command and control. And that means it can't be stolen. No one can heist your drive, inspiration, vision, judgment, values, or personal emotional mechanics—the ingredients that (as *Do More Faster* reminds us) make product and service ideas come to life and make a business succeed.

Damn the Torpedoes—Competition Is Good

So what if others decide to execute on your idea as well? If you believe in your team and your mission, this is *not* a stopper. In any good business category there will *always* be competitors, but they will produce a different result than you do. It'll look differently, perform differently, and be formulated differently for all the "great news" reasons we just mentioned (because their drive, inspiration, vision, judgment, and so on are all totally different from yours). If one start-up car maker in Japan and another in Arizona both come up with the idea of making a hybrid sports coupe and they execute with the same degree of commitment and technical skills, their prototypes are sure to come out looking like two kids from different mothers. There's room in the market for one or both to succeed.

In fact, having competitors is always better instead of worse for your own chances. Competitors help build bigger, more-aware markets than you can do all by yourself, and attract customers you can tap when you prove you are the number one choice.

The idea of renting server space to computing-hungry companies wasn't a one-of-a-kind, original idea when Rackspace got started in 1998. There were already competitors who were far more established and had millions in revenue (versus Rackspace's zero). But the company founders believed they could find customers willing to rent server space from them in San Antonio. They figured they could carve off a piece of a growing market by finding a way to do it faster, better, or cheaper. They eventually overtook the other players in the category, not because they were the only ones with the unique idea, but because of the unique way they executed on the idea, adding value in services and support that set them apart for their customers.

Fool's Gold

So from now on, stop worrying about having the perfect, fail-proof idea and quit obsessing about someone stealing the one you've got. Never let your quest to perfect your idea before you start keep you from getting started. That pipe dream is for amateurs, because no guaranteed idea exists without you adding the magic ingredient: your entrepreneurial skill and your power to dare and do. And as we'll see, no idea can get perfected until it's exposed to the reality of customers in a real market.

The Best Ideas

So what kind of idea should you be looking for if not the perfect one? The answer is simply the one that sparks you enough to get you into the game. A catalyzer that flips your switch and gets you and your partners going. You do need a business idea—one that promises to fill a need or creates a new opportunity for which others will pay you money—just not the *perfect* one before you start.

Here's some distilled-over-time wisdom to help you identify a good business idea.

1. The Best Ideas Are the *Small* Ones   Love the good, small ideas, the ones with the fewest moving parts. These are the kind you can set up and demonstrate to customers at an early stage, adjust until you have a Minimum Viable Product (MVP), determine if people want to buy it from you for more than it costs to make, and see if they'll come back for more or tell someone else to buy it. Then you can grow the business.

(By the way, in the pages that follow, we'll be referring frequently to the "product" you plan to offer. Of course, your business might just as well be built around the intangible, personal kind of product usually referred to as a "service." However, it's wordy and clunky to keep repeating the phrase "product or service." So whenever we say "product," please remember that we are really saying "product or service.")

If you think about it, Netflix was a simple idea: "We're going to send you movies through the mail and never charge late fee." Enterprise was a simple idea: "Rent cars to people where they need them, not at the airport." Kayak.com took all the travel sites and put them on one screen. Rackspace said we're going to have IT guys set up and maintain a bunch of servers, then rent space on them.

Mrs. Fields simply started with a chocolate chip cookie recipe she liked. She baked some and found out people would pay for them and ask her for more. That's a small business. Then it made sense to open one store. If she found out she could get enough people to buy cookies to cover the cost of her business—that is, rent, ingredients, and her own salary, for starters—her store could sustain her. Then she could start opening more stores just like it.

Small ideas are so great because they let you discover whether they work or not in the shortest amount of time for the least money. Nobody knows whether any idea will work—least of all your biased self—until a customer who isn't your mother or your best friend volunteers to hand over a hard-earned dollar, giving up the opportunity to spend that dollar on something else.

In fact, here's a bonus pearl of wisdom gained from people in what used to be called the mail-order business (they invented modern advertising) and in the movie business, who have been trying out new ideas for a hundred years—and this is sage—

"Nobody knows anything."

In other words, nobody knows whether any idea will work until the market votes for it by buying it and recommending it to their friends. Never trust anyone, no matter how senior they appear, who tells you they *do* know. If they did, they would be billionaires. And if the billionaires who own movie studios know what would work, then the dozens of big-budget movies made by the most experienced professionals in Hollywood with A-list actors and directors that flop every year wouldn't.

Remember this when you're tempted to believe a "nega-holic" who tells you your idea will never work before you've created a real prototype and sold it. The only sure thing is the idea that worked. Small ideas let you find out faster, one way or the other.

On the flip side, large ideas are the ones that require you to account for 15 independent variables that need to fall into place for your business to work. Those are the kind we avoid and you should, too. These are the ones that require you to build a network that doesn't exist yet, or create a whole new infrastructure before customers can use it. A legendary example of this was Webvan.com, widely recognized as the number one business disaster of the original dot-com era. Webvan was an online service that would deliver basic goods like groceries to your door within 30 minutes of your call. The idea in those days was that all you needed to succeed on the Web was "first mover advantage," meaning the head start on market share enjoyed by the first company to jump into a new industry; pesky things like sales, revenues, and profits were not required.

Webvan raised hundreds of millions from the most sophisticated investors in the world: Benchmark Capital, Sequoia Capital, Goldman Sachs, and more. They hired a CEO from a renowned consulting firm. They spent $1 billion to build a central distribution center that required them to invent one-of-a-kind automated systems for their model to work. They bought a huge fleet of trucks and built a presence in 11 major cities. Among 10 other things, their model required them to disrupt the behavior of the American consumer, who had been happily buying groceries at the friendly local supermarket for over 50 years and didn't feel he or she had a problem that Webvan could solve. And they did all this *before* they knew whether their idea would work with customers.

What a surprise it must've been when they found out it didn't. At all.

For a dozen unanticipated reasons.

As usual, the SEALs have the right idea. "Crawl, walk, run" they say. Take a good small idea and get it to work really, really well. *Then* make it bigger.

Here's another way to look at it, to help you keep your ideas small . . .

2. The Best Ideas Do *One* Thing Really Well   Good ideas fix one problem or provide one new benefit the customer didn't have before. They do not solve every customer problem and revolutionize every part of an experience. In fact, the opposite is true. Nobody, except the gadget geeks who design TV remotes, wants a device that does 157 things. They want a product or solution that does one important thing very, very well. They want it to solve a single nagging problem or provide one cool new opportunity for a price they feel comfortable paying.

(By the way, about pricing: Most people are fair and reasonable and have no problem paying a tad more if they perceive new or enhanced value. Come in a little lower? Fine, that's gravy. But not too low—then it starts looking a little suspicious.)

Vast fortunes are made by letting customers do one thing better or with less pain. Generations of parents stabbed themselves when fastening diapers using safety pins. The market was transformed and a giant business was created when someone put two Velcro strips on each side of the nappy, capturing millions of customers overnight.

Do you own a couple of gas stations? Try this change: clean the restrooms. Really clean them, every day. (Include a vase of plastic flowers and a $9.95 fake painting on the wall, too.) That'd be enough to draw traffic to your station instead of all the others at the intersection. We have to give big companies credit where it's due: ExxonMobil did this and motorists did beat a path to their door. We know people who will drive out of their way every time to go to their stations, even if they don't need to use the restroom.

Want to know what Rackspace did that no one else in the industry had tried?

When customers called, they picked up the phone after one ring.

It was proof of a promise of customer service you could hear and see. Their one thing was Fanatical Support.

Throwing a barrage of features at savvy customers and investors is more of a problem than a solution. It impresses no one. It means you can't focus, can't commit, can't specialize, and can't get the big thing right. The added bells and whistles become a blur of irrelevance if not annoyance. Suppress this urge.

3. The Best Ideas Are 1 Percent Better   Shoot for a real, obvious, and dependable 1 percent difference. You can always go up from there. You don't need to create a giant breakthrough like Apple's iPod to succeed; in the real world, success occurs by tiny fractions. The difference that wins an Olympic gold medal is .001 seconds. And you can be crowned the best golfer in the world when you win the right tournament by the length of a single putt.

No one ever reached for the second-best product on the shelf. When people have a choice, and aren't already locked into one technology or one supplier because they've made a large prior investment, they just pick the one they think is better—by any margin. Best by 1 percent is the tipping point, and it can change the world. When it comes to better, an inch is as good as a mile.

The key is that it needs to be a difference that is obvious to buyers—one that they can measure, feel, or easily see demonstrated.

It needs to be something the customer can appreciate—something important enough to care about and trusted enough to believe.

It just has to relieve 1 percent more of my pain or deliver 1 percent more opportunity or delight in my life. It only has to be 1 percent lighter, more compact, simpler, more dependable, friendlier, harder, warmer, or colder. Whole companies have been created because someone reduced two keystrokes to one, or built a dustpan and brush that snap together, or mixed the ice cream in front of you at the counter, or made real handmade espressos rather than plopping a capsule into a machine.

But your 1 percent has to be a real, meaningful difference, and that's a term of art—not just a claim, a variety, a slogan, or a choice for its own sake. It has to add a specific value. What makes a meaningful difference in the world or advertising and marketing is a critical notion that will get its own discussion in Chapter 10.

4. The Best Ideas Inspire You   They guys at Rackspace succeeded because they found a difference customers wanted that others weren't willing to provide. Fanatical Support sometimes cost the company a little more money and work to deliver, but Rackspace provided it every time, rain or shine, until customers started to believe it was the difference that the company stood for.

But—and it's a crucial *but*—Rackspace was able to give its customers what they wanted only because it gave its people—the Rackers—what *they* wanted. Here's how Graham Weston explains it: "We decided at the beginning that what everyone wants from work is to be a *valued member* of a *winning team* on an *inspiring mission*. And we decided we would do everything in our power to build our company that way. When given this kind of opportunity through work, people will give their hearts and minds to the team and the mission day and night, not just their backs and their hands from nine to five. People will tap their entrepreneurial power for the cause at every level of the company. It's a competitive advantage money can't buy."

But this is easier said than done. To give your people an inspiring mission to fulfill, you have to start with an idea that quite simply inspires *you*, because it's the easiest kind—actually, the only kind—you can use to genuinely inspire others.

The idea doesn't need to be fancy. And that doesn't mean to pick your favorite pastime outside work. You're in search of a business, not a way to relax on Saturdays. It has to fill someone else's need. But the prospect of owning and building out this idea needs to excite you and incite your enthusiasm. Then it will motivate you and the other members of your team because your ability to bring it to life will advance your values—social, technical, artistic, or financial. Depending on those values, you might be as excited to open a new bicycle shop or invent a new way of providing small business accounting services as someone else might be to build the first civilian space station or cure global hunger. It's 100 percent up to you. Either way, as long as your excitement is genuine, it will be contagious.

So, of the dozens of business ideas you might pick, don't settle for one that doesn't inspire you in some way. Not just because it's more fun, but because in the tougher, scarier moments that all missions periodically create, you'll renew your strength and commitment by tapping into this energy source. And most important, you'll pay it forward to all your teammates. Don't leave an asset this precious on the table.

5. The Best Ideas Make It *Easier* or *Faster*—Not Cheaper One final word: you can *never* lose or waste your money by making a product *easier* or *faster*. You'll never meet a customer or a consumer who doesn't want these two features. All other performance and properties being equal, customers will reach for your product if it has them. Of course, the overall value still has be there. Drivers would rather own a BMW that can do 80 mph than a Kia that claims it can do 120. But in general, when your idea makes some activity measurably faster and easier without trading off some other key element, like safety, or maybe luxury, or indoor plumbing—your idea is a good one.

Notice, however, that we didn't include "cheaper" in this rule. Cheaper is the oldest motivator for consumers, but if you're not careful, it's the oldest, deadliest trap for your idea and your business, too.

Cheap is not an idea; it's a condition. As a main difference in any category, cheap*est* is a club with one member. You're volunteering for a never-ending fight to stay there because customers who are loyal to the cheapest will never be loyal to you. It makes your brand one-dimensional and extinguishable in a day by any competitor who cuts his number below yours. It's out of your control. And while customers will always be looking for cheap*er*, they'll also always be reluctant to accept what cheaper usually means: lower service and poorer quality. Promising cheapest without lowering quality is a recipe that will seduce customers once. It's bad for both of you.

Price is one whole side of any business equation and your idea should include the fairest price possible. But don't make price your cornerstone. Hang your hat on faster or easier—or any of the other timeless human values, like smarter, sexier, safer, or more dependable. Leave cheapest to Low Price Lenny, and see how long he lasts.

WHAT ALL BUSINESS IDEAS MUST DO

A business idea is different from other ideas in one respect: it makes a customer a promise. From the customer's perspective, the promise is to fix something, solve something, take away something bad, or give me something of greater value for one purpose: *to make my life better*. Specifically, to make me safer, sexier, healthier, richer, or more secure, popular, successful, or comfortable.

In return, I will pay you money. It's a service contract.

When you're looking for a good business idea, you're looking to fill a need, take away pain, or add some pleasure—and that's it. It's never more complicated than that. The people who are good at coming up with these ideas ask simple questions of themselves and others, and they practice a lot. The more they look and ask, the more they see.

They ask these eternal entrepreneurial questions:

- What pain or problem can I take away?
- What new experience can I give?

They get the answers by listening, observing, being open to possibilities, and perhaps most of all, asking themselves the "What if?" and "Why not?" questions.

- What if there was a way to do _____?
- Why can't I get _____?
- How come no one ever fixed _____?

It's not a matter of cleverness as much as inquisitiveness. The folks who ask these simple questions most often come up with the most answers.

Then the question becomes: Is it feasible? Is it possible? Possible for *me*? This is where the physical mechanics overlap with emotional mechanics, and the answer throughout the ages is: nobody knows but you.

Ninety-nine percent of human progress was impossible—except for the one person who decided to do it. But that's why you're an entrepreneur—remember?

- Idea, people, and execution: each is worthless without the other.
- Even if you had the perfect idea (which you don't), the world couldn't care less about it because . . .
  - All ideas change once they hit the reality of the market.
  - What the world pays for is ideas that are executed.
- Competition is good.
- The best ideas are the ones that:
  - Are "small"—they work without too many moving parts
  - Do one thing really well
  - Do it 1 percent better
  - Inspire you so you can inspire your people
  - Make it easier and faster—not necessarily cheaper
  - Promise to make my life better by taking my pain away, or giving me an opportunity I never had

---

7

The Big Picture (Continued)

People and Execution

PEOPLE

Saying "Your idea is worthless" is not to nullify the importance of great ideas, but to drill in a point. Of course turning ideas into action is what entrepreneurship is all about. But there's another factor, as big as any idea you'll ever have, that controls the future even more. And this is meant in the most real, hard-asset, non-touchy-feely kind of way.

More vital than any idea you'll come up with are the *people* you'll come up with to bring your idea to life. Ideas are nothing but static, dormant non-things until people make them tangible, adaptable, executable, and saleable. People are the only machines on earth that can perform this entrepreneurial alchemy by turning a concept into something concrete.

Here's what the great entrepreneur turned investor Yossi Vardi said to us about it when we were chatting in a Tel Aviv coffee shop:

> When someone comes to me with [a] big nondisclosure agreement
> to sign, I tell them, "I'm sorry, but you need an investor who is much

cleverer than me, I wish you luck." They sometimes can't believe this. They look at me like I'm crazy and say, "But how could you not be interested in the world's most amazing idea?" And I tell them, "I couldn't care less about your idea. In fact, I don't even want to know what it is. Because between now and your being successful enough to get customers to buy it, it may change 20 times from what it is today. The only thing I know that I am buying that won't change, is you and your partners; what you care about and your ability to solve problems. I don't invest in ideas."

And then he added, "When they come in with another partner or two, it shows me they can at least get along with someone other than themselves. You can come up with an idea as a loner, but not grow a business. What's the ideal number of founders? I'd say three, maybe four."

So what matters most in an entrepreneurial venture is the founding talent, the quality of the people who run with the idea, no matter what it is. And it follows that if one smart, capable, hungry person (that's you) is good, three or four are always better, so long as they have the character and craft to be true teammates.

FOUNDING TEAMS ALWAYS HAVE AN EDGE

It can't be said enough times in this book: Teams are the ultimate multiplier for success that there is. True teams, that is—particularly in entrepreneuring.

Ask the Beatles. According to legendary guitarist Eric Clapton, "Their magic was that they were four guys who played like they were one." Or ask the SEALs who operate in four-man teams and who will tell you, "In battle, individuals die. Teams win." Your chances of executing your idea—adapting it, fixing it, shaping it, and selling it—go up exponentially when you do it with a small true team of founders, two to four to be precise. David Cohen of TechStars points out that about 95 percent of the start-ups that are accepted into their summer mentoring programs come in as founding teams, not individuals. It just makes sense; three brains that are as focused on the mission as you are can come up with many more ways to accomplish it. They make you smarter and more observant, save your ass when you screw up, and help save your idea's ass when it fizzles on the launch pad the first few times. They also enhance your ability to survive the emotional ups and downs of risk, obstacles, and temporary failure, and the attendant fear that accompanies these things.

You of course are person number 1 in your own career. And on day one, you may be by yourself. Not every entrepreneur is lucky enough to have a small team of talented, trusted associates ready to embark on the journey with him. That's okay. You may come up with that first great insight for a new business idea when you're thinking by yourself. Many of the world's great ideas started that way—with one person alone in the car or the shower.

But you should be seeking that founding team from moment one, asking, *"What's my idea? Who's my team?"* equally if you plan to create a successful enterprise, not just a product innovation. It's that important.

Dan Brodsky-Chenfeld, a world-champion team skydiver and specialist in the art and science of team building, says that champions whose fortunes live and die with the success of their teammates have their radar turned on at all times to identify potential new teammates, the same way an entrepreneur might be attuned to new ideas. They mentally keep candidates on file, even if the need for a replacement team members might be years in the future. People with the right stuff simply don't come along every day.

──────

PEOPLE AND CULTURE, DAY ONE

Beyond you and your founders, your primary people sphere extends outward to include employees, associates, vendors, and customers. Every day, the actions these people take for or against you decide whether your business will succeed or fail. How they vote with their dollars is 100 percent their choice—not yours.

None of these people's wants and needs are an add-on at the end of your business plan. They are the heart of it. Your idea is about them. It exists solely as a vehicle for improving their lives and to make them love you.

That's how they see it anyway. And they hold the only votes that count. Otherwise, they have a million billion other ideas and businesses they can choose to do business with. They don't need yours.

GIVE BEFORE YOU GET

Thus you must first and always give customers what they want before you can hope to get what you want. Likewise, you must spend your best quality time thinking about what customers want before thinking about what you want. Success will be directly proportional to how often and how consistently you do this.

And if you honestly and truly devote your time and energy to serving your customers, they will reward you in greater proportion. They will give you their trust, their repeat business, and they will tell their friends about you. Some will become partners or seek to work for you. This little gem of business insight was worth the whole price of a famous little book called *The One Minute Sales Person:* "I have more fun and enjoy more financial success when I stop trying to get what *I* want and start helping other people get what *they* want."[1] Spencer Johnson and Larry Wilson called this success secret the *Wonderful Paradox.* And over the years, I've never seen it fail in the real world—whether you're selling one-to-one or marketing to a huge customer base. You'll find over and over in your career that some version of this paradox works in almost every aspect of business that involves strategy, tactics, and human relations—from creating your product specs to your branding to customer care.

It works because it's the law—customer law. *Other people's* hearts and heads are the only place your success resides. Your product, reputation, and brand are not what *you* think; they are what *they*

---

[1] Spencer Johnson, *The One Minute Sales Person: The Quickest Way to Sell People on Yourself, Your Services, Products, or Ideas—at Work and in Life* (New York: William Morrow, 1984).

think. You are only as good as they deem you to be. The main thing to store in *your* head is this paradox.

WHAT EMPLOYEES WANT

The Wonderful Paradox applies to employees just as much. They want what everyone wants: to enjoy the chance to be respected, trusted, and honored—really, to be loved—by participating on a team that has a chance to touch greatness. When they do, they give it all back to you—plus a whole lot more. The best summary of this (repetition is good) is they want to feel like (1) valued members of (2) a winning team on (3) an inspiring mission. Keep providing this trio of benefits and your employees will give you back what money and compensation cannot buy: everything they've got, right through to the best entrepreneurial parts of themselves. When employees get it, they'll want to love you back, and their primary way of showing it will be by loving your customers. And that's huge, because once you've proven you can perform as promised, being loved is something customers really, really like.

Culture is the catchall word for a work environment that either delivers or doesn't deliver the emotional benefits employees want. A company culture is nothing more than a distinct set of values made real by actions each day. The best cultures follow the universal rule of simplicity; that is, they have the smallest number of very important values, not a laundry list. All cultures start from the top down. Therefore, you should know exactly what kind of culture you stand for—and that you will make real no matter what—on the day you open for business. This super success secret is free, entirely in your hands, and entirely on your head if wasted.

WHAT CUSTOMERS WANT

At the start, customers only want one thing from you: a solution they can't get anywhere else that's worth the price they are willing to pay for it.

Despite what you may hear from new-age business gurus, *they do not want a relationship with you*—just like you don't want a relationship with every stranger you meet on a bus or a blind date—until you show them you're trustworthy, reliable, competent, smart, have their best interests in mind, and are fun to keep around. *Then* they will readily bestow a relationship on you and love you back. And that's the gift that keeps on giving. They will talk about you, recommend you, try to protect you, even cherish you, because good relationships are, after all, what life is all about.

The shortest distance to customer love is through employees who are receiving the same thing from you. You cannot expect your people to respect, care for, and put your customers first without receiving the same from you. Sure, there are exceptions where companies who don't love their customers get to serve them anyway; look at today's airlines. But the reason we keep using the old legacy flyers is that they hold a near-monopoly on an essential service and we have no choice but to get in line and hope. We'd jump to any alternative the second we could. Hence the amazing rise of Southwest Airlines—the first airline to make appreciating customers the bedrock of its brand.

In short, a business model that makes your customers feel disrespected and resentful is no recipe for success.

There are myriad reasons why humans instinctively collect good relationships while scrupulously trying to avoid bad ones. It derives from the primitive instinct for belonging to the group and loving our families. And it comes from the brain's love of shorthand and low energy output. An established relationship means my brain doesn't have go through the whole fight-or-flight, positive-or-negative reaction every time I deal with someone. Once we can mark a relationship as familiar and safe, we can relax and function with a single click.

So, it's fair to say that in any category where there's a need, customers are indeed open to a potential relationship. You just have to keep your promises, perform, and prove yourself worthy first.

In other words, give before you get.

WHAT EVERYONE ELSE WANTS

Nobody ever creates a successful enterprise all alone, without some support and effort from other stakeholders along the line. Beyond employees and customers, you'll have relationships with vendors, community members, and others who can either contribute to your success or undermine it. All will respond to the Wonderful Paradox.

A wise person once told me, "What people remember is how you made them feel." They will give you their money in return for goods and services. But they will give you their feelings in return for the way you care and how you show it. Those feelings build brands, reputations, and success stories.

The key insight is that customer connection isn't rocket science. People merely want to be happier, healthier, safer, richer, more attractive, and more successful—and to feel trusted, respected, and important to someone. Exactly like you.

EXECUTION

Execution refers to every tangible action you take to create and manage an enterprise, from designing and building your first prototype to selling and distribution, hiring the right people, training them well, and managing your cash flow. The skill with which you do all these things and more is the measure of your talent for execution.

Entrepreneurs will always need to dream. But put a simple Doer with a grasp of the mission in competition with a Dreamer with a PhD and a ton of research and the Doer wins every time. Execution is the "making something out of nothing" part of entrepreneurship, and without it, success doesn't exist. The ability to execute faster, better, and cheaper is the Entrepreneur's timeless, unshakeable advantage over Optimizers everywhere. It's the reason there will always be a place for you, why big companies will secretly be afraid of you, and why you'll have a chance to carve out a market, compete with the big boys, and even overtake them down the road. It will always look at the start like the big fish have all the advantages, and indeed, they have resources, respect, and reach that you can only imagine. But they'll never have what you have: the fear turned into fire, the inspiration of the mission, the need, the yearning, and the emotional mechanics.

Bureaucracy makes Optimizers love process and research over products and results. Entrepreneurs can take more creative risks to solve problems because they have nothing to lose. They are fast and nimble because they have no cumbersome control layers holding them back. That's why no one can conceive, adapt, and execute like a hell-bent entrepreneur.

A lot of the specifics we'll talk about in the next section will overlap into execution. There are also whole libraries of books on specific areas of execution, from financial planning and facilities management to customer service and R&D, for when you need and want to get into strategic and technical detail. Our purpose here is to give you the rules of thumb that apply to execution of anything.

THE LAW OF THE LASER

Focus

"Don't fear the man who has practiced 10,000 different kicks. Fear the man who has practiced one kick 10,000 times." Legendary marketing author Al Ries uses this example in his book, *Focus: The Future of Your Company Depends on It*:

> The sun is a powerful source of energy. Every hour the sun washes the earth with billions of kilowatts of energy. Yet with a hat and some sunscreen you can bathe in the light of the sun for hours at a time with few ill effects.
>
> A laser is a weak source of energy. A laser takes a few watts and focuses them in a coherent stream of light. But with a laser you can drill a hole in a diamond or wipe out a cancer.

Your ability to execute is directly proportional to how well you focus your energy and your team's energy, as narrowly as possible, on just one or a very small number of most important things. The heart of the matter is holy for all who execute: first seeing it, then sticking to it. The competitor focused on a single, simple, clear objective always wins. Always.

Successful teams can define their objective in just a few words:

- Our job is to deliver Fanatical Support.
- Our job is to fix the way the world sits.
- Our job is to get the ball to break the plane of the goal line.
- Our job is to find and kill Osama bin Laden.
- Our job is to design and manufacture the ultimate driving machine.

Remember, a single clear goal is what customers want most from you as well. They don't want your product to offer a laundry list of features. They know instinctively that jacks of all trades are masters of none. They don't want you to give them everything—they want you to give them one thing and to do it better than anyone else in the world. If you do, customers by the millions will choose your product, whether it's the sharpest razor, the most durable roof shingle, the most accurate wrist watch, the most booming bass notes, or the driest martini in town.

So test yourself constantly. Your biggest job as executor-in-chief is to keep peeling away the distractions and maintain your focus on the smallest number of most important things. This is a universal law.

A Fast B+ Beats a Slow A . . .

A great entrepreneur from the Greatest Generation used to say, "Work, work, work. Think later." What he meant was this: always *default to action*. Analysis and research are important, but they quickly lead to diminishing returns. Once you're in motion, the reality of market cause and effect will always force you to make critical changes, to adjust your course, and change your plan. You learn 10 times more in the process of doing than in the process of deliberating and deciding. So err on the side of getting your idea out there, prototyping your product, publishing your paper, aiming and firing at your target, and then making adjustments for wind, elevation, and distance until you start hitting it again and again.

This explains the huge historical advantage enjoyed by Internet-based entrepreneurs. They're able to prototype a software product fast and inexpensively with little capital investment, then float it in the marketplace and start learning. A couple of geeks with laptops are able to find out in virtually no time whether anybody wants their product, will pay for it, loves it, or hates it because prototypes expose benefits, mistakes, unknown unknowns, and unintended goofs. This concept of achieving "validated learning" as quick as you can by putting out a Minimum Viable Product (MVP) as soon as possible is probably the greatest insight you can take away from Eric Reis's best-selling book, *The Lean Startup: How Today's Entrepreneurs Use Continuous Innovation to Create Radically Successful Businesses*.

Remember, since "nobody knows anything," access to the tools for rapid prototyping in technology start-ups is a God-given gift you do not want to waste.

. . . But Not Too Fast

Now it's time to qualify the paragraph above, and this is very important. As Einstein said, "Everything should be made as simple as possible—but not simpler." Get into action and the market fast, but not too fast—not until your product can provide customers with its main benefit. How do you know when you've reached this critical point? The key words are *Minimum* and *Viable* in Minimum Viable Product, or MVP.

Think of this as the minimally floatable boat. Or the minimally stay-able hotel. Don't ask the market to try your boat until you've built one that can carry a couple of passengers without taking on water and sinking. Don't sell rooms in your hotel until you've got sheets on the beds and working toilets. Don't open your restaurant until you have enough wait staff to get my cheeseburger to the table while it's still hot.

The market starts forming its opinion of you, your brand, your promises, and your value the minute you ask for an interaction. You don't get too many chances to blow it with them in the beginning. And word travels from one customer to another really fast. So don't invite the town to come out and watch the first flight of your flying machine until it is an MVP—which means that it can get reliably airborne, at least for a few seconds. But don't wait until it's as powerful as a 747 either. Just make sure Version 1.0 minimally works.

DATA MAKES YOU DUMBER

Too much data, that is. The human brain runs on an ancient rule of thumb that says, "In an emergency, take the first right answer and go!" When your life is on the line, don't wait to find and weigh a better route to safety because by the time you do, you'll be the tiger's second course.

This rule of fast and frugal applies to execution as well. The right answer is often astonishingly obvious and presented to us early. Of course, it's always prudent to double-check your thinking to eliminate dumb and easily avoidable mistakes. But then, if indeed we are erring on the side of action, we should decide and act. This is how Entrepreneurs do it. We emphasize trial, not striving for absence of error.

Here's a major difference between Entrepreneurs and Optimizers. Both are equally likely to stumble across the right answer to a pressing problem. But then, on principle and for the sake of process, the classic Optimizer will refuse to act on the obvious until he has conducting a mandatory sequence of data collection, research, and committee hearings designed to insure against any possibility of a mistake. Time and time and time again, we've watched too much data become the great Optimizer trap.

Awash in data, Optimizers eliminate any sense of expert intuition and common sense. They kill momentum, obscure the obvious, and make basic judgment mistakes in a fruitless effort to scrub every decision clean beforehand.

Timing, it turns out, is everything when it comes to too much data. The curse occurs almost always *before* the fact, when you rely on pretests to do what research can't and shouldn't do: predict the future, prescribe success or failure, or, God forbid, design your solution.

But *after* you've built and tried your prototype in the real environment—now that's a completely different story. Now you are tweaking, adapting, and learning to improve. Now you're free to gather all the data in the world. But do this *after* you launch, not before.

The data trap also bedevils the creation of business plans. All the same rules apply. Only the market can validate your plan. Work, work, work, and think later. Or put another way: if you overthink, you stink.

PRACTICE WITH LIVE ROUNDS

The Navy SEALs undergo a constant system of rotation that goes like this. At any given time, about 650 SEALs are deployed somewhere in the world. About 650 are actively training for the next mission. And about 650 are in the process of returning and regrouping from the last mission. That's a very small force. Yet in one recent year, the SEALs expended more live rounds (bullets) in training than the entire U.S. Marine Corps!

There are two points here. One is that the SEALs are so good because they train and practice their craft relentlessly, more than anyone else. The other is that, when the SEALs practice, they do everything possible to simulate the real emotional and physical experience of being on a live, life-and-death mission. This concept is so critical, they're willing to put themselves at risk during practice to mitigate the risk and maximize success in actual battle.

Believe it or not the SEALs use live rounds when training for close quarters combat (CQC), the kind of house-to-house fighting required to attack Osama bin Laden's compound and conduct modern urban warfare in general. Live rounds sound different, feel different, and produce far different consequences when mistakes are made. You don't even think about training this way unless you know your teammates are the best in the world and you can trust them not to kill you with a stupid move. When you finally step through the door in Abbottabad, Pakistan, with terrorists carrying automatic weapons inside, it's no first-time shock when the firing starts. You've been there, felt that. You and your teammates know in your gut that you can execute successfully in the "kill house."

What the SEALs are doing with this kind of practice is much more than planning, preparing, and thinking. They are *prototyping*. They are testing and tweaking their product in conditions as close to reality as they can get. They are building an MVP version of a successful CQC assault; then they are trying it over and over to get data on what does and doesn't work, where the strong points and weak points are. After weeks of this kind of work, they know they are the best in the world at executing because of this relentless dedication to prototyping until they get it right. It's their way of controlling their own destiny and mitigating risk and failure.

Getting your MVP into the real world and watching it perform in marketplace conditions is the entrepreneurial equivalent to practicing with live rounds. Seize the opportunity to prototype under the most authentic conditions you possibly can, whenever you can. And never pass up an opportunity to interact with real customers. Their feedback—good, bad, or indifferent—is your only way of knowing whether your product is likely to survive under battle conditions or instead blow up in your face.

———

ASK, ASK, ASK IS HOW YOU RECEIVE

Execution sounds like it's all about finding solutions. But getting there in the first place is all about asking questions—a few, specific, obligatory questions over and over. This can be repeated to you enough.

In his book *Mastering the Rockefeller Habits*, author Verne Harnish summarizes three fundamental principles that business titans would agree are key to success. You ready?

1. Have a handful of rules
2. Repeat yourself a lot
3. Act consistently with those rules (which is why you better only have a few of them!)

Sounds rather familiar, doesn't it? (Of course, it's the principle of three or four and the system of heuristics, couched in slightly different language.)

The rule of repetition governs every aspect of Accelerated Proficiency as it does with every worthwhile task in nature. To execute, we follow rules. But what we repeat are not the rules themselves per se, as much as the *obligatory questions* the rules make us ask in order to stay on course. We take these questions from a mental checklist, just like a pilot judging his approach to the runway. We align through a constant series of mini-tests, which are simply a set of specific questions that ask where we are at that moment, relative to the guiding principles. Just as a pilot would ask, "Am I on heading? Is my speed right? Is my descent rate right? Is my power right? Is my pitch right?," we ask the mini-test questions over and over and over again until touchdown.

This is all we do when we execute. But to make it work, it's vital that we stay focused on asking the right questions. And that's the subject of our next chapter.

PEOPLE

- Founding teams rock. The other half of the eternal question "What's my idea?" is "Who's my team?"
- The universal people rule is: Give before you get.
- Think about culture starting on day one—and every day thereafter.
- Employees want to be valued members of a winning team on an inspiring mission.
- Customers want a relationship, but only if you keep your promises and improve their lives.
- It's not complicated. All people want the same things: to feel happier, healthier, sexier, richer, stronger, safer, more important, or more needed—exactly like you.

EXECUTION

- Remember the law of the laser: Focus.
- Avoid gathering too much data before trying your prototype in the market; it will make you dumber. After you launch, feel free to gather all the data you want.
- A fast B+ beats a slow A.
- Simulate the real world in practice as much as you possibly can.
- Have a handful of rules. Repeat them often.
- Mini-test your alignment frequently by asking your core questions.

8

The UnStoppable Six

*How to Run a Billion-Dollar Business
or a Start-Up the Rackspace Way
(in about an Hour)*

EVERY BILLION-DOLLAR BUSINESS begins as a scrappy small business.

Rackspace once had 3 employees. Now it has 5,000. Watching something that starts so simple and straightforward turn into a global enterprise so big and complex furnishes another insight that underlies just about everything in this book.

The insight is this: The core of any business, the original heart and soul that first allowed you to succeed with customers, never really changes for companies that stay vibrant and relevant, no matter how big they get. Inside that billion-dollar corporation, the value equation you first discovered is still just as simple—and most important, it needs to be, if you want to keep going and growing. The selling proposition that made them choose to buy from you—the values, the dream, the reason the market needed you—is still the foundation of it all. The idea you stand for must be reaffirmed by the decisions you make and actions you take every day.

This truth is as important to you as a start-up as it is for the biggest companies. And it's based on an immutable concept called the Piper Cub Principle.

THE PIPER CUB PRINCIPLE

This little rule should boost your faith in what's possible at any stage of growth because it applies in so many areas—from building things to operating things to designing things or just understanding in general. I heard it from an airline pilot who flies the Boeing 747–400ER—a plane that weighs 910,000 pounds, carries 400 people, and is as long as a city block. A Piper Cub, by contrast, is a tiny two-seater airplane whose first models had a 40-horsepower engine that looked like it belonged in a cartoon. Original Cubs were so basic, they didn't even have a radio or a gas gauge.

The 747 captain told me that when he's at the controls and gets in a jam, especially during training, he reminds himself, "Inside it's just your little Piper Cub, pal—stick and rudder, power and pitch. Flies the same."

Indeed it does.

The Piper Cub Principle offers two big parallels for starting and growing anything, and at the same time affirms Accelerated Proficiency:

1. Inside even the most complex-looking systems there's a simple process you can grasp very quickly.

2. Operating a complex system usually comes down to just a few very simple, fundamental controls that you simply have to repeat over and over.

Inside that massive 747 is a virtual Piper Cub that takes off, flies, and lands according to the same techniques and principles. And you control that 747—not just virtually but actually—with the same stick, rudder, and four instruments you'd find in a Cub, monitoring your airspeed, altitude, power, and compass, and keeping them all in balance. Those are the same four elements that are essential to fly any plane. That's why, without exaggerating, if you can fly a little Cub, we can teach you to fly a $350 million 747 in less than an hour.

Today's most sophisticated jets have the four instruments displayed on two TV screens on the instrument panel (a.k.a. the dashboard) right in front of the pilot. The one on the left has the flying info—the airspeed and altitude just mentioned. The one on the right has the navigation info so you can get to your destination. The whole airborne monster with 400 people riding in the back is flown from just those two screens.

The Piper Cub Principle is the reason why a billion-dollar business and a small start-up fly the same way. If you can manage one, you can manage the other.

THE UNSTOPPABLE SIX

Like the pilot's handful of essential instruments, what we call *The UnStoppable Six* are the six essential priorities—three strategic and three tactical—that are the master principles you need to start up and run a successful, belief-based enterprise like Rackspace. They reflect the principles that Graham Weston and the Rackspace founders used to get ahead of their competitors and still use today.

As leader of your enterprise, you too will use a very small number of key instruments as your guides, constantly cross-checking and making adjustments. These are the *daily questions* you ask yourself on day one and every day thereafter, over and over again, to stay in flight and get where you're going. You can share this duty with others on your team. But if you're the CEO, you cannot delegate it. Too many CEOs nowadays try to hand these essentials off to surrogates. And their brands and businesses fly into the ground as a result.

The UnStoppable Six are organized in two sets of three: the *Strategic Three* and the *Tactical Three*. Balance these two sets, maximize them every day, and your business can fly—first as a Piper

Cub, manned solely by your founding team, and later as a jumbo 747, with hundreds or thousands of employees and customers around the globe. The Strategic Three are Difference, Team, and Customers. The Tactical Three are Famous, Product, and Revenue.

Now let's go into a bit more detail.

THE STRATEGIC THREE

1. Difference

Your *unique difference* is what sets you apart—the benefit your customers believe you give to them that nobody else does. Hence, you are their *number one choice* when they have a need for what you do. The difference must be a simple, measurable, and of obvious value to your customer—whether you sell a product or service, pipes or perfume. The more complicated it is to explain, the less of a real difference it usually is. Far more companies succeed with a difference in *one specific thing* than with a long list of generic things.

Finally, your difference is what your customers perceive and say it is—not what you hope or pretend it is. Without a real difference, the market really doesn't need you.

2. Team

Like a SEAL team, your entrepreneurial *team* will consist of the people who have signed on to your entrepreneurial mission. They are steeped in a culture of values, rules, and traditions that you as the founder create. They vote on your success with their hearts, minds, souls, and energy, providing your business with its richest possible competitive advantage. Since team members own these assets outright, no leader or dictator can control them by anything but voluntary means. But team members give them freely, beyond any monetary consideration you can pay, when they are treated like valued team members who belong to a mission that matters. Being needed in this way is one of the most basic human instincts. Satisfy it and people will respond in kind by loving their company and their customers.

Finally, nothing is a greater multiplier of value than the synergy of a true team. When a true team is in action, 2 + 2 may equal 400,000.

3. Customers

Customers might as well be air and water; your business has no life without them. Success is something you must learn from them because only they can teach it to you, through what they need, where their pain and pleasure are, how they want to be sold to, what kind of relationship they want to have with a company in your category, and so forth. Customers hold the answers to all your most important questions about your product, service, and brand. The Wonderful Paradox is that the secret of getting what you want is to think most about what *they* want.

For you, the trust of customers is your ultimate prize. It's the must-have for anyone who wants to achieve entrepreneurial success. Nobody buys without it. The greatest businesses never stop learning how to succeed with their customers. Then they do one more thing. They perform. Always.

THE TACTICAL THREE

1. Famous

There's that age-old question: If a tree falls in a forest and no one is around to hear it, does it make a sound? If your product is the greatest idea in the world but nobody hears about it, will you sell any? I don't know about the tree in the forest, but I can guarantee the answer to the second question:

No.

No business succeeds without customers, and nobody can be your customer if they don't know your offering exists. Your job as a start-up is to build a working product that has a unique difference, get someone to pay you more than it costs to make, and build basic awareness—that is, get people to notice you among a hundred billion other products, services, and messages that whiz by every second in our hyper-communicated era.

Thus, your job is to execute on getting famous—in your neighborhood, your town, or your industry. You get famous by using marketing to develop a unique reputation—also known as your brand—and through actual, physical selling, which generates the revenue without which no business can exist.

There are many methods for getting famous: advertising, promotion, public relations, endorsements, events—and, today, social media, which is basically word-of-mouth (the most powerful fame vehicle of all) on steroids. There are a few big secrets and techniques in each method that can effectively boost your chances to get more for less money. These are the techniques that all great brand builders have employed, and you can, too, starting on day one. We're going to cover them when we talk about branding and sales.

For now, just know that your job isn't done when you come up with that better mousetrap, it's just beginning. You've got to think seriously every day about how and why you're going to get famous.

2. Product

Put a basic working prototype into potential customers' hands as soon as you humanly can. We call it the Minimum Viable Product (MVP)—a product that actually works, for a price someone would actually pay. It's as simple as that. And you have absolutely nothing but a pipe dream until you execute on this moment of truth.

The reason is that *nobody* knows anything ahead of time—and you can learn this right now the easy way or find out later the hard way. No brilliant venture capitalist, analyst, or fortune-teller knows whether you and your partners can succeed with customers until you have built an actual, tangible unit of value that a person with a need can try and buy. There are just too many known and unknown variables in people and markets to do anything else but build it, float it, test it, and if it even partly works, adjust it and improve it. If it doesn't work, you can pivot to a better idea or plan with the least loss of resources.

The longer it takes to get to a MVP, the greater your risk. There are whole industries devoted just to reducing the time, expense, and risk of reaching MVP, like the CAD/CAM industry, which lets you create computer simulations in color and 3-D so you can virtually test your prototypes. As we've discussed, the speed, ease, and affordability of creating prototypes in industries like software is one of the huge blessings of the digital age.

But don't feel discouraged if you're not a geek or software developer. The world needs entrepreneurs in a thousand different disciplines beyond iPhone apps, and each one has its risks and rewards. People start new hotels, retail stores, even new airlines all the time. Prototyping is more complicated and costly in these fields than in the software business—but it can be done. The key principle remains the same: do it as fast and as cheaply as you can, and turn product version 1.0 into your springboard for a endless series of improvements based on market feedback. That's how you get from an MVP to a world-class, world-beating offering.

3. Revenue

This one is the key for entrepreneurial start-ups.

Remember our minimally floatable boat? Well, now think about a minimally flyable airplane like the Wright brothers built, which did one thing no other glider had ever done: it stayed aloft. It only did for 12 seconds, but that's all it needed to prove the MVP and change history. All the Wright brothers had to do was aim for that basic milestone, then revise the prototype from there—not aim to build the Space Shuttle.

Think the same way when it comes to revenue. Once you get yourself to the break-even point, you've broken the barrier, you've become a going concern—you're a living thing. Now you can grow.

"Just break even" is one of the sagest pieces of entrepreneurial advice you'll ever hear from veterans of the process, because it simplifies your team's first financial mission. It aligns your little picture and your big picture. For now, your big picture, when it comes to revenue, is breaking even.

To get there you'll focus on the little picture: Sales.

BUSINESS PLANNING: MAKE THE
UNSTOPPABLE SIX YOUR TEMPLATE

The principles behind the UnStoppable Six will guide you in another big way. They give you the quick-step framework for vetting your ideas and setting up a business plan by lining up the obligatory questions that lead to the right solutions. You must always check and re-check the Strategic Three and the Tactical Three, and force yourself to give the simplest answers in the fewest words.

Here are the six essential questions that are raised by the UnStoppable Six:

Q1. *What is our unique difference?* What's the *one most important thing* we'll do that nobody else does? Why does the market need it? What specific pain do we solve? What new opportunity will we offer? Is our difference a nice-to-have or a must-have? Who are the competitors in this category now and what exactly do they offer?

Q2. *Who is our team?* Do we inspire each other and admire each other? Do we make each other stronger? Do we have a greater skill set together than apart? Do we share the core values that will become our culture, and can we all articulate them today?

Q3. *Who are our customers?* Who and where are they today? How are they solving this problem without us? What's most important to them? Do they know they have this need or do we have to educate them to recognize it? How will our offer match their need? How do they want to be sold? Who is serving them now?

Q4. *How do we get famous?* What's our name, our brand, and our language? How do we spread the word without breaking our start-up budget? How can we look a little larger than life? How do we get people talking about us? Who can we partner with to help us reach the world?

Q5. *What's our Minimum Viable Product?* What's the smallest, simplest, fastest, and most affordable working system we can build that proves our concept? How do we begin to execute it starting on day one?

Q6. *How will we get revenue?* How will we get enough to break even? How exactly will we sell? To whom will we sell? What's their purchasing cycle? How much must we sell in what amount of time? Who on our team will lead this effort? How does the market buy now? How much do they pay? What is our price?

Learning is the basis for any team or organization to answer these questions. Continuous, enthusiastic, open-minded learning. (It has to be continuous because the answers will keep changing.) Then, wherever you can, simplify with a vengeance. Learn and simplify and pass it on.

It's not rocket science. It's repeat science.

Asking the questions is your job as CEO, just as it is for the jet pilot watching those screens. They are the questions all the founders, and ultimately, your whole team should be asking.

Now let's get to the specific skills and rules we need to learn in about an hour.

- Inside most complex systems is a simple fundamental truth—the key to the lock that never changes. Inside a 747 is a Piper Cub.

- The experts are simply the best at the fundamentals and repeat them over and over.

- The UnStoppable Six are the key indicators for flying any successful business, big or small. They're divided into two groups: The Strategic Three and The Tactical Three.

- The Strategic Three are DTC: Difference, Team, and Customers.

- The Tactical Three are FPR: Famous, Product, and Revenue.

- Think of them as your daily questions, the ones you ask over and over to keep your mission on track to succeed. Use them to guide business planning as well as to shape and inform your moment-to-moment operating decisions.

9

Everything You Need to Know about Your Unique Difference (in about an Hour)

When you ask experienced business people what a *difference* is, it's amazing how few can actually tell you. They react like it's a silly question, then they offer up a slogan, a generic claim, a piece of puffery, a nuance, or a cliché—anything but a real difference.

And yet a real business difference is the most important distinction you'll ever make for your career or your company. A difference is not just a word, it's a term of selling science, a condition of measurable value, the reason potential customers think you will take away their pain or make their life better. It's a perceived distinction that persuades me to buy; in other words, it's *a selling difference*.

If you want to be an entrepreneur, you want to be able to discern a genuine, meaty difference in your sleep. In commercial

119

enterprises—in capitalism itself, where customers have free choice in the marketplace—this is the center.

A selling difference is the one thing that's most unique, important, and memorable that only you offer, that makes you the number one choice versus your competitors. It's the tipping point of customer choice because it tells the world you're the *only*, the *most*, or the *best* in their price range.

Whether the difference is 1 percent or a 100 percent, it doesn't matter—remember, an inch is as good as a mile when it comes to winning—so long as it's obvious, important, and believable to the customer. Your difference sets your business apart and sets you up for success.

A true difference benefits you in three ways: it guides how your product is designed and will perform, it guides how customers perceive you, and it guides what you tell the world that will make you famous. All three add up to *what you stand for* in the customer's mind. And that is the definition of a *brand*.

––––––

SPECIFIC IS TERRIFIC

If you take away one practical tip from this chapter that you can put to use tomorrow, it should be this: real selling differences are almost always *specific*. There's no easier rule to implement for a lower cost and a higher yield that will sharpen your difference and help your brand get famous.

Put actual differences up next to puffy slogans and you can really see the contrast.[1]

"20 percent lower rates because *we* make the loans" is a difference. "Engineered to Amaze" is a slogan.

"Seven Whole Grains on a Mission" is a difference. "Bursting with Goodness" is a slogan.

"We give you Fanatical Support" (which you then prove by picking up the phone on the first ring) is a difference. "Your call is very important to us" is a slogan.

––––––

[1]Based on branding guru Jack Trout's famous question: "A difference or a slogan?"

"America's number one 4G network" is a difference. "Passionate about better coverage" is a slogan.

"15 minutes saves you 15 percent" is a difference. "The insurance company on your side" is a slogan.

"100 percent fresh, never frozen" is a difference. "Now that's good eatin' " is a slogan.

"Tulsa's most popular tranny shop, 'cuz transmissions are all we do" is a difference. "We treat transmissions right" is a slogan.

After reading a few of these examples, think back to the commercials broadcast during the most recent Super Bowl (if you can still remember them, that is). You may notice that many of today's richest, most sophisticated advertisers don't seem to have a clue about what their difference is or how to express it. They spend millions on ads that provide customers with no idea who's even selling to them, let alone why in the world we'd possibly need them. They seem to be in thrall to gurus and soothsayers who think that selling the product is the least important part of the advertising experience they are creating.

Well, let's be clear: it's okay for them to waste billions of dollars on frivolous puffery, but it's not okay for you. As a budding entrepreneur, you can't afford it—in fact, you can't afford to waste *any* of your scarce and precious resources (of money, time, and energy) on vague, non-specific messages. You need a real difference to tell the world about in the clearest, most penetrating terms, and you need it the day you open for business.

You need it because for customers, the Unique Difference is what your business is all about. If not, what is the point? Customers don't care that you need the business to feed your family. They care that you're offering them a Unique Difference that solves a problem—one that's worth risking their hard-earned dollars on.

NO DIFFERENCE? THEN YOU'RE A COMMODITY

Without a difference, you forfeit the big strategic advantage you should have as a nimble, creative, problem-solving entrepreneur. You're now a commodity and that means you no longer have customers, you have *counterparties*. You've conceded that they can buy something of equal value from any of your competitors. And when that happens, your only hope is to have the lowest price. You're like gasoline: a legal definition, not a differentiated product, and certainly not a true brand. It's a brutal position to be in if you want to control your own fate and rise above the pack.

Graham Weston spent time in the cattle business when he was growing up. He discovered that the livestock industry was based entirely on efficient production. You tried to minimize your costs, then you went to market and the price you got was what you got, even if it was far less than what you'd spent during a year of hard work. You had zero discretionary power to control customer preference by creativity or risk, and no way to otherwise outwit or out-service your competitors.

That's what happens to you when you're stuck in a commodity business.

Graham learned from the experience that price minimization is really value minimization. When he joined Rackspace, he and his partners made sure that the company was built on a difference they could design, improve, and adapt from day one, rather than hoping to cut corners and somehow turn themselves into the low-cost provider. They established standards and values that enabled them to serve customers in a way that set them apart. Having a Unique Difference has helped them escape commoditization and the business dead-end it inevitably implies.

THERE'S *ALWAYS* A DIFFERENCE—IF YOU KNOW WHERE TO LOOK

Every business has a true selling difference in waiting if you know where to look. As an entrepreneur you're already granted a differentiating head start, simply because you are a unique individual who brings a unique set of eyes, life experience, perceptions, and passion to whatever product or enterprise you create. Entrepreneurs have found ways to differentiate practically everything under the sun. Nike differentiated Air, Florida differentiated sun, Perrier differentiated water. Kentucky differentiates the grass its racehorses eat. Idaho not only differentiated potatoes, it differentiated dirt.

But identifying your Unique Difference isn't always obvious or easy. The masters of differentiation, the makers of the great brands have spent decades perfecting the secrets of distinctiveness. Add the timeless rules that follow to your bag of tricks and you'll find a difference that sets you apart no matter what business you may be in.

In fact, you're going to find that most of the time, companies have *too many* differences to choose from, not too few. The answer is so often the one that's obvious to everyone but you, simply because you're too close to it. You may have 10 great differences to choose from. Your job is to identify which one is the most distinctive. Then you have to commit to it and stick to it. It's one of the hardest choices any business leader ever makes, but also one of the most important.

ANATOMY OF A SELLING DIFFERENCE

The most powerful difference is always *one thing* that sets you apart from others—not two or ten features jammed together. It's *one* attribute that's important to the target customer, one thing that you do best, most, or only. It can be any one of a hundred attributes: the fastest, the healthiest, the most durable, the most reliable, the most attractive, the sexiest, the safest, the most prestigious, the largest, the strongest, the lightest, the best priced, the most energy-efficient, the most authentic, the softest, or the hardest. *The safest* tire. *The fastest* human. *The only* shoes that breathe. All great brands originally built themselves on a single proposition like this and they still do. That's because the masters know a rule of thumb for differentiating called . . .

THE ONE ITEM OF CARRY-ON RULE

Today our senses are assaulted with about 500 billion messages a minute. But the human brain has a defense mechanism for handling this chaos that it's used since prehistoric times. We call it the One

Item of Carry-on Rule. Here's how it works. Out of the barrage of features and benefits and details a seller might throw at us about a product, our brain stubbornly chooses just one to remember—the one idea it deems most interesting and important—and that's the one we file in the overhead bin. All the rest get left at the curb. By a series of unconscious shortcuts, heuristics, and gut feelings, we instantly surmise the heart of the matter, so we're ready to make snap decisions and take emergency action on the least amount of information. When time is of the essence—like when a saber-toothed tiger used to decide we looked like lunch—this is a basic survival strategy.

As entrepreneurs, our job is to tailor our message to work with the One Item of Carry-on Rule. That means that, in today's hypercommunicated world of choice that too often blurs into a sea of sameness, our first order of business is to find the one unique, important, and ownable "best" that sets our product apart. If we choose the right difference (and if our product then performs as promised), they'll love us for it.

There is a name and a structure for this very critical idea that differentiates your business. It's called a *Dominant Selling Idea.*

YOUR DOMINANT SELLING IDEA

A Dominant Selling Idea (DSI) is your single most important advantage—the one item of carry-on your customers will choose as their primary reason to buy.

A difference needs five ingredients to be a DSI. You must ask a prospective difference to stand up to these simple tests. It must be:

1. *Superlative.* It says you are best at an attribute or number one at something—the *best* choice for a specific need.

2. *Important.* What you're number one in has to be something that *matters*— something I really want or would want if I knew about it. A must-have, not a nice-to-have.

3. *Believable.* There has to be a unique, plausible reason *why* you claim it is superlative and important—a reason that makes logical sense. It can't be trusted if it's not credible.

4. *Measureable*. It must be *specific* and *obvious* in its performance. It must be totally aligned and consistent with all your claims. You must prove your difference every time you perform. Remember: *What's measured matters*.

5. *Own-able*. It can't already be taken by somebody else. It must be uniquely available to you, so you can stand for it.

A DSI with all five attributes is the heart of what brand marketers call *positioning*. A position is simply the place you own and occupy in the customer's mind that nobody else does. It's the center of gravity we'll build from when we get to talking about making ourselves famous through branding.

Seeing the Dominant Selling Ideas All around Us

DSIs are everywhere. The more you notice them, the better you'll get at crafting your own. In the days when TV and radio were undisputed kings of the media world, broadcast advertisers were brilliant at carving out and expressing DSIs, many of which have lasted for generations. Like:

- M&M's: the little chocolate pellets that come with a shiny shell in pretty colors so *the chocolate doesn't rub off and make a mess . . .*
- Wheaties: cereal so nutritious, it *makes you a winning athlete . . .*
- Hall's Throat Lozenges: the ones with unique, *nose-clearing menthol fumes . . .*
- Timex watches—the *most durable watches . . .*
- Pork—It's *a lean, white meat like chicken . . .*
- Volvo is *the safest car . . .*
- BMW is the car with the *best German engineering . . .*
- Rackspace has *the world's number one customer service* in the cloud . . .

Now, please note—the italicized words are the Unique Differences expressed in everyday language for a few famous brands. It may be that, as you read the list, your mind was whispering you, repeating some familiar phrases: "M&M's Melt in Your Mouth, Not in Your Hand," "BMW is The Ultimate Driving Machine," "Timex Takes a Lickin' and Keeps on Tickin'!," Those are the catchy taglines for these differences written as Micro-Scripts—those remarkable story-telling phrases that your mind loves to remember and repeat. When a Micro-Script conveys a DSI, it packs a branding punch that is difficult to match.

Advertisers used to be great at writing unforgettable "elevator pitch in a phrase" Micro-Scripts, and you can too. You don't need to have an ad agency and a big marketing budget. Some of the best Micro-Scripts in the world are written by everyday entrepreneurs who have nothing more than a true love of their product and their customers.

At Rackspace, the Micro-Script for "the world's best customer service in our business" is "Fanatical Support." If you go to the company website, you'll see pictures of Rackers who've won the Service Person of the Year Award. What they get to put on and wear proudly in front of all their cheering teammates, like the yellow jersey in the Tour de France, is a real live straightjacket—a vivid (if tongue-in-cheek) emblem of the sheer insanity required to live up to that unique and unforgettable tagline.

Graham Weston remembers the origin of the phrase: "Fanatical Support is an expression of our difference that has guided our decision making every day since Racker David Bryce shouted it out for the first time at a company rally over 10 years ago and everybody cheered. It wasn't a fancy ad agency creative who came up with it. It was just one of us, a team leader who happened to love his company, his product, and his teammates. Our contribution was to hear it and recognize it, that's all."

If you're listening carefully to employees, customers, friends, and stakeholders, you'll hear great language that can be turned into taglines and rallying cries, too.

We'll talk more about this kind of UnStoppable language in Chapter 12, when we discuss how to make yourself famous.

The Smartest Marketers Still Use Dominant Selling Ideas

Many criticize the modern mavens of meaningless marketing (none more than we do), but there are still superstars who emerge with strong, clear DSIs and have the meteoric market share to show for it. These are the folks who love the idea of standing for a crystal-clear difference in the mind—and are savvy enough to say so.

Here are some modern-era DSIs for brands you've probably noticed:

Splenda—Made from Sugar So It Tastes Like Sugar

Geox—The Shoes That Breathe

Kashi—Seven Whole Grains on a Mission

Geico—15 Minutes Saves You 15 percent

U.S. Post Office—If It Fits, It Ships

Cialis (the 36-hour ED pill)—When the Time Comes, You'll Be Ready (it also comes with two bathtubs in the woods)

And here are some other DSIs you can spot just driving down the road: The *fastest outboard engine*, the *real New York style bagel place* (in Bangor, Maine), the *unbreakable line of laptops*, the *highest mileage hybrid*, the *online dating website for lawyers*, the *only organic local farmer's market*, and the *shoulder surgery specialty group*.

There's an amazing amount of selling information contained in each of those DSIs. Each one provides potential customers with a great reason to buy.

The point is that devising a DSI for your product isn't brain surgery. It's something much simpler yet even more important—brain *singularity*.

Remember, Without Performance You Have Bupkis (Nothing at All)

Not all products with a DSI can boast a big budget and a famous tag line. But every one *must* deliver consistent performance as promised that proves the difference through tangible action, no matter what.

Without it, your difference is hot air and the perception of your product in the customer's mind (which is equivalent to your brand) will be hot air, too. With it, you can often succeed without advertising it all. Your customers will do the talking for you . . .

Volvo is the legendary safe car. Recently, Volvo became newsworthy again because the century-old company was named by 70 percent of consumers as the world's safest car in a global survey—despite the fact that the "safe" tagline hasn't appear in an ad in decades! The DSI is kept going by the word of mouth. Customers and mechanics still talk about features like the famous "steel safety cage," and the fact that Volvo has been unilaterally responsible for most of the big safety innovations in cars since its inception—from the three-point seatbelt to antilock brakes. And I read a little while ago that they're keeping the legend alive by announcing a company-wide mission to build an injury-proof car by 2013.

That's a 100-year-old heart that's still differentiating, folks.

Since we're talking about cars, Toyota is "the car that doesn't break." Not a bad DSI. This one has never been in their advertising or their tagline. (Few people actually remember any of their taglines.) But after polling all 27 Toyota owners in the neighborhood, talking with three local mechanics, and hearing everyone lead with a version of the same idea—"they never come in for repairs," or "they easily go 300,000 miles," or "they don't break," or "only Hondas even come close in reliability"—the point was installed in our heads and is now being passed along to others.

And Starbucks, the brand so many gurus (used to) love to talk about, used neither a tagline nor any advertising at all during its historic rise. All they did is show up on every street corner and in every mall and bookstore—and perform. They featured a European-style coffeehouse atmosphere and coffee selection. They created their own branding language, using words like Venti and Grande. And they not only let you sit there for hours, they encouraged you to do so without feeling guilty. They gave you free Wi-Fi. After your home and your job, they wanted to stand out in your mind as "your third place." You walked into and sat down in the Unique

Difference at Starbucks. They lived it, and to millions, the proof was obvious.

Starbucks's epilogue: Eventually, because a cup of java at Starbuck's was so expensive (some people refer to the chain as "Four Bucks"), because they opened too many stores too quickly, and because they started cutting corners on things like latte preparation, Starbuck's DSI began to morph in a lot of customer's minds, and their business began a historic dip. They now appear to be bringing it back.

The story just shows that no difference can rest on its laurels these days. *It's the job of the CEO to monitor the UnStoppable Six every day.* Your difference is too fundamental to your survival for you to delegate it to surrogates.

What If Someone Else Already Owns the Unique Difference You Want?

In other words, what if you check and someone is already number one in your category? What then?

It's a problem faced by UnStoppable differentiators every day—and the solution is simple.

If someone else is already number one in your category, you have to adjust your specialty to the right or left and *invent a new category* to be the best in.

For instance, if there are already three regular dentists in town, become *the children's* dentist and you'll be instantly set apart. If there are five children's dentists, you may want to be become the children's orthodontic dentist.

Enterprise Rent-A-Car became the biggest rental company in America not by trying to be a me-too entrant in the airport car rental category, but by carving out a new category: "The rental car for when you're not at an airport." In fact, as a symbol of their difference, because they knew your car might be in the shop and you have no way of getting to their lot, Enterprise told the world "We'll Pick You Up." Call them on the phone right now and they'll repeat the same tagline.

Choosing Your One Unique Difference out of Many: The Tests

Remember, your big difference is not every feature and benefit in your value proposition—it's simply the one thing you're best at that's most interesting and important to the customer.

To begin with, if you can fill in just one of these blanks in your category, you're potentially looking at your superlative attribute, the first of the five DSI ingredients:

The best at _____.

The one (or *The only* one) that/with _____.

The most _____.

The number one in_____.

Then, you have to test for the other four ingredients. Is your big attribute of major importance to your target audience? Is it believable for you to say it? Is it true? Do you prove it every time without fail in a measurable way? And last, is it own-able, or is it already preempted by someone else?

The answers to these questions will tell you whether you've uncovered your DSI—or need to keep searching.

HOW RACKSPACE DISCOVERED ITS DIFFERENCE

The founders of Rackspace tried two versions of a Unique Difference in their category of renting computing space on servers (later called managed hosting), before getting it right on the third try. Luckily for them, they knew they *had* to find their Unique Difference, and started their quest it on day one; once they found it, they focused on it with a vengeance. Graham Weston recalls the process:

"Finding the difference we could stand for was such a priority, that within the first month of opening our doors, we spent the money to travel from Texas to Connecticut to meet with the legendary differentiation expert, Jack Trout, co-author of an original book called *Positioning: The Battle for Your Mind*. Jack was a great mentor in forcing us to focus as though we were already a great big company with a superior brand.

"Although we didn't have terms like *Dominant Selling Idea* then or its five ingredients, that's the process we followed until all five fell into place for Rackspace.

"The first difference we tested we could call, 'Customized, dedicated servers for geeks and techies who could save money because they wouldn't need *any* customer service!' It's hard for people who know us now to believe that we started out as the 'you trade a low, low price for no, no service' company at the beginning.

"Problem was, when you put it up to the superlative, important, believable, measurable and own-able test, it failed on superlative and own-able. There were competitors who could and did make the exact same offer of dedicated servers. So we tried a new big difference after a few months.

"The second position we tried was, 'Internet Servers Made Simple,' the classic 'we're the ones who make it easy' strategy. We even created a software tool on our website called the configurator that let techies set up their own servers online, an innovative idea back around 2000.

"Again, we found we couldn't hold onto ownership of this position long term. Customers could easily build configurators themselves and match our ease-of-use claims.

"And then, we found the DSI that customers told us they wanted. Amazing to us at the time, it was the opposite of our first assumptive position.

"It happened when some very irate customers who had had major technical problems, but were unable to get the service they needed, called us directly and slammed us for it.

"It was the dawn of the obvious. The industry's me-too standard was to offer little or no service, assuming techies could handle it. But there are always problems with technology. Bigger, more sophisticated companies with critical-mission websites needed to find a provider who they could trust for superior, 24/7 service, and when they found it, they would pay for it.

"Nobody in the industry was offering it. It was expensive to deliver, difficult to implement, and thus wide open for us to own. Investors and experts told us it was foolish to buck the tide and risk the added cost. But our key customers were saying the opposite.

"So we took what was then considered a big entrepreneurial risk. We knew we had to go all-in or nothing to make world's best customer support believable and tangible for the industry. We bet our company on it. Not long after, our focus on this difference brought us the words Fanatical Support, which no company that was not as committed to service as we were ever would have adopted as a tagline. But we did, because we knew then that that's who we were. Before long, the industry knew it too—and Rackspace really took off."

We've shared Graham's story at such length because it illustrates several of our key principles, including:

- Ideas and differences change.
- Entrepreneurs need to be adaptable.
- Learning to succeed with customers is paramount.
- Daring pays dividends.
- Once you find the center, hold onto it come hell or high water.

It's also important to see that finding that one big difference is vital not only for what you do—your product and your performance—but for what you're going to say that makes you famous and turns you into a great brand. So your Unique Difference has an overlapping function that ties together the Strategic Three and the Tactical Three.

THE UNIVERSAL PARADOX

Paradoxes abound in the world of The UnStoppables, just as in life.

The paradox when it comes to positioning (i.e., finding your DSI) comes down to this:

The narrower you focus your difference *and* your message, the bigger your difference grows and the wider your message goes.

The fewer things you say in each speech, the more you are heard.

The more specific you are, the more generally your benefit gets applied.

Why? Because being number one in one thing, like safety, is not only easier to remember and repeat, thanks to the One Item of Carry-on rule; it also brings reams of other positive associations along with it, like quality construction, superior technology, genuine corporate caring for customers, and so on.

Win the gold medal in one Olympic event, and the world will naturally assume that you possess a wide array of athletic talents. Finish fifth in half a dozen events and no one will remember your name.

OTHER PEOPLE'S HEADS ARE ALL THAT COUNTS

Once you determine the Unique Difference for what you're selling, you have to make a challenging claim or a great promise to let the marketplace know it exists (i.e., to make it famous), or you'll be that proverbial tree that falls in a forest that no one hears. Indeed, the difference is only a claim, an *invitation* for customers to think about the product the way we'd like them to, until we actually perform and deliver as promised. Only then is the difference marked, trusted, and accepted into the customer's mind.

And the customer's mind isn't just the most important thing for your business—it's the only thing.

Your brand—which is the perception *and the belief* that you have a meaningful difference—does not come into being when a customer sees your advertising about a difference. It happens when the customer tries your product and experiences delight, relief, or satisfaction—when they feel the racing suspension in the BMW take the curve, get the help they need for a technical problem at 3:00 AM, or walk into the smell of fresh bread in the middle of Grand Central Station at Zaro's Bread Basket bakery. That's when your difference takes hold and becomes a brand because it's superlative, important, believable, measurable and own-able in the customer's mind.

Anywhere you look you'll see organizations whose managers go around breathing their own fumes, assuming their DSI is one thing, when going out and talking to customers would reveal that, in their minds, they stand for a different idea altogether. It's a perilous position for a company to be in. What might be circulating with customers is a dominant *un-selling* idea. Ever heard Nieman Marcus jokingly referred to as "Needless Mark-up"? Or Whole Foods called "Whole Paycheck"? Both are big, successful brands, but to the customers who pass along these nicknames to their friends via word of mouth, they stand for overpriced merchandise, not glamour or a unique retail value as they might hope. This yawning gap between the DSI they want to own and they one they really have is a problem they need to address it ASAP.

Friends, your big selling difference is in the eye of the beholder. That had better be your customers *and* your valued teammates and employees. If you want to be UnStoppable, then other people's heads are all that counts.

- People tend to remember one thing. The One Item of Carry-on Rule states that people tend to remember only one thing.
- A true selling difference meets five tests:

  1. Superlative: it's best at something.
  2. Important: it really matters to the customer.
  3. Believable: it makes sense coming from you.
  4. Measureable: it's obvious to see; "What's measured, matters."
  5. Own-able: it's available for you to be number one in the category.

- Specific Is Terrific.
- The 3 Rs: repeat, repeat, repeat.
- The Unique Difference lives in other people's heads, not yours.

You must think about your Unique Difference, what it is that keeps you the number one choice of your customers, every single day. It's the direct responsibility of the CEO and founders in any successful company. It's called a Dominant Selling Idea.

10

Everything You Need to Know about True Teams (in about an Hour)

The greatest compliment one SEAL can bestow on another is to call him a teammate. In the sea underwater at night when it is the darkest, it is your teammate who swims beside you, always ready to provide you air if you run out, untangle your line if you're caught under a ship . . . In the air, it is your teammate who checks your parachute before you jump . . . [and] lands beside you in enemy territory. On the land, it is your teammate who walks your flank, covering your six . . . And sometimes it is your teammate who lays down his life for yours.

—*Admiral William McRaven, honoring SEAL Lt. Michael Murphy*[1]

---

[1]Daniel Klaidman, "For Navy SEALS, The Biggest Threat May Be Hollywood," *Newsweek*, November 5, 2012, http://www.thedailybeast.com/newsweek/2012/11/04/daniel-klaidman-the-seals-biggest-threat.html.

YOU ARE A SMART, AMBITIOUS PERSON with ideas, talents, unique life experience, and a fire in your gut that's greater than your fear of trying. This makes you UnStoppable.

Now imagine you times four.

Think of how the four of you could brainstorm solutions, overcome obstacles, and take on risk and fear on any mission if, indeed, you all still acted as one.

You'd be making yourself into a new organism (something, as you'll learn, like a SEAL team). An engine with just one cylinder could be made from the most advanced components in the world. Yet all you'd have is a lawnmower. But put four or more cylinders together and you have a Ferrari, a powerhouse that goes 180 mph. All you did is multiply 1 times 4 and make a team that will work in concert to fulfill one mission: to turn that crankshaft.

As a team you become far greater than the sum of your parts. You may have multiplied your power by 4 or by 400,000, but either way the synergy still bumps you up to a whole new league.

I've said on several prior occasions that teams are probably the ultimate multiplier of human potential in the pursuit of anything. No single lesson was emphasized more by the great practitioners I encountered during my journey to the heart of entrepreneurship than this one. It's why the world's ultimate doers on the most trying missions work *exclusively* in the framework of teams. They study the art and science of teams; they nurture, encourage, and flat-out demand that any individuals who qualify to serve will form themselves into, and only think of themselves, as teams and teammates.

But not just any kind of team. Not the kind of team that's been given lip service by innumerable corporate Optimizers—the superficial kind of team thrown together by happenstance or by an arbitrary management fiat.

I mean true teams, a concept the founders of Rackspace discovered by bare entrepreneurial necessity long before Graham Weston and I got to know about SEAL teams or any other example from the outside world. (Graham said it to me this way in one of our conversations: "You know, we were instinctively putting together our own kind of SEAL teams inside Rackspace without realizing it.") As an entrepreneur, you too will need to harness this power and put it to work for you, because a true team can take ordinary people and make them into champions. And it can take champions and raise them to a level of potential they could never have achieved in this world on their own. No individual, no matter how talented or adept, can compete with the exponential intelligence, creativity, ability to withstand challenges, and pure power of a true team.

Like each element of the UnStoppable Six, team is something the entrepreneurial leader needs to think about continuously. In this chapter, you'll learn why and how.

THE ROOTS OF SMALL, SUPER-POWERED TEAMS

It's no exaggeration to say that SEALs and Israeli commandos veritably worship the power of team and its effect on missions and personal survival. "In battle," they say, "individuals die, teams succeed." Team function is a strategic, tactical, and emotional issue for these warriors; it's a must-have in the world's riskiest, most dynamic environments. For all the same reasons, it's a success accelerator for you as an entrepreneur.

Teams can be any size, of course, but for our purposes, we'll be talking about a default team size of four—the primary functional unit that the SEALs and Israelis use in operations, based on decades of experience and team research that shows there is an inherent workable balance and proficiency in this number. A four-person SEAL fire team includes a commander and three specialists. Not coincidentally, this is a common number for many of the most successful founder teams we see in start-ups today. It's not a mandate, just a good solid model. After all, the Beatles were the Fab Four. Do you need any better or more enduring model of creative global success?

Like Krav Maga, true teams are built on a few simple principles that leverage human instincts we've all been expert in since birth. Teams are powered by a universal social impulse to belong, to be needed by others we care about, and to feel important because we are valued by others.

As biologist Edward O. Wilson explains in *The Social Conquest of Earth*, the need to be part of a group is hardwired so deeply, it provides a new way to understand evolution:

Group selection is just as important as individual selection—"The human brain evolved to be intelligent and social at same time," ruled by the amygdala and other emotion centers. [There's that pesky amygdala again.] People yearn to be in the best groups—then discriminate against outside groups, judging opponents less likeable, trustworthy, even human. Fans at sporting events are lifted by seeing their group's symbols—cups, banners, uniforms, etc. and repelled by opponents'. Our unconscious impulse is to divide into groups swiftly and decisively, to join and to belong. "Group selection lifted us to solidarity, genius, enterprise. But also to FEAR." Fear of being humiliated and ostracized by the group, fear of not belonging, fear of losing the group's love and approval and most critical—fear of losing the group's protection which is vital for our survival. "Group instinct" creates the best in us—we reward altruism, selflessness, courage—but also the worst in us. We can be prompted to go to war at the slightest provocation, forgetting any of its past consequences.[2]

These drivers are far too powerful to ignore, to resist, or on the other hand, for us not to seize as our multiplier if we are to be the best leaders, citizens, or entrepreneurs.

━━━━━

TRUE TEAMS

I realized it wasn't the world championships or the trophies and lord knows it wasn't the money that made me commit my heart and soul to that 4-way team. I just loved being needed so much by three other people that I had such incredible respect for. I would've done anything not to give that up.

—*Dan Brodsky-Chenfeld, six-time group skydiving world champion, author and lecturer*

---

[2] Edward O. Wilson, *The Social Conquest of Earth* (New York: Norton, 2012).

True teams leverage it all: the emotional mechanics of membership and belonging, the yearning for a higher cause, achievement, and trust—and the love that passes between those who are needed by one another. A company that understands and values this potential will build a culture of true teams from day one. Teams and the value-based culture that sustains them go hand in hand.

What Special Qualities Define True Teams?

The following are the ideal qualities you would find on any sports or military team that operates at an elite level. Inside companies, team dynamics can approach these ideals, too, and can yield extraordinary results—as long as members are given the respect and the authority to follow an inspiring mission.

1. True Teams Function as One Machine, One Organism Each member feels like a vital part of that organism, without whom the others can't succeed. As they practice together, their individual expert intuitions blend and are elevated into team intuition. Consequently, the team members function smoothly and seamlessly together, trusting their lives to one another's ability to do their jobs. In CQC (or "close quarters combat," the military term for house-to-house fighting), after hundreds of hours of team training, SEALs describe their movements together as a flow: "It's like a hockey game, but almost graceful, like a ballet—we communicate without words, we know where our teammates are going and where they'll be without looking." Others have described it as a "four individuals with a single beating heart."

2. True Teams Build on One Another's Strengths Members of True Teams admire one another's talents and strengths. They build one another up, augment one another's performance, sacrifice their own comfort, and root for their teammates because it's the only way success is possible. They may criticize, but they never tear down, exploit, or control by fear. Leaders must believe it's a privilege to lead and put their people first. But when they do, their people will love them back and follow them through hell.

The love of belonging and performing for one's peers is among the most powerful incentives that compel human action. It is more powerful than money or individual reward. It motivates people to take the risks needed to innovate, even endure far higher levels of physical pain than any individual would endure on their own. It makes true teams UnStoppable—the most powerful force for achievement on earth.

After the Beatles broke up in 1969, each of the four team members went on to forge a career as a solo artist, with some commercial success. But none of the four created a body of work as memorable, popular, and influential as the music the Beatles crafted during their brief time as a team. Why? A major reason is that the three songwriters in the Beatles—John Lennon, Paul McCartney, and later George Harrison—stimulated, inspired, and challenged the others. Every time Lennon wrote a new tune he hoped to break new artistic ground and so surprise and impress his band mates—and he worked and reworked his songs longer and harder in pursuit of that goal. It was the same with McCartney and Harrison. After the band broke up, these three artists were left on their own, and the relatively disappointing results they achieved reveal that something big was missing: the magic of the team.

3. They "Follow Like a Leader"   Although team members always subordinate themselves to the leader, they're always aware of the big picture/little picture on their own, so they can add intelligence and corrective action should the others miss an opportunity or a threat.

It also means that if the leader is out of operation, the other members can step up and lead as needed because they understand the mission upward and downward.

4. True Teams Shift Leadership on Demand   True teams are flat, informal organizations that transfer authority to whichever specialist team member is "up" in any phase of the mission. When the task is demolition, the explosives specialist holds authority for that piece of the operation and is deferred to—even by the commander. When the sniper or the mini-submarine driver is up, authority for the maneuver goes to that member. Such informality and flexible authority is only possible when these values are burned in from a larger culture. The SEAL ethos says, "We expect to lead and be led. In the absence of orders I will take charge, lead my teammates and accomplish the mission. I lead by example in all situations."

5. True Teams Run on a Simple, Clear Set of Values Anyone Can Articulate   This is the larger organizational culture. It's reinforced by a unique language, symbols, and traditions that represent the proprietary bond among its members.

6. True Teams Are Not Formed or Assigned by Management Decree   To quote a world champion I know, "True teams choose themselves." There must be a standard for admission that matches the standards of the group. Members and leaders are either accepted and respected, or ultimately ejected. But all of this happens based on the decisions of the team members themselves, not on orders from some outside expert or boss.

If you want to wield the power of the true team for your entrepreneurial mission as its leader or a founder, you must create an environment and a set of values that enable it. You must promote an UnStoppable team culture with values, standards, measurements, and traditions right from the start.

HOW AN UNSTOPPABLE CULTURE NURTURES TEAMS

True teams don't spontaneously appear any more than plants germinate without soil. They require what we have already called a Belief Culture—to some, another of those soft, amorphous terms that don't belong in business. But in UnStoppable organizations like the SEALs where teams are practically deified, the culture that advances and sustains the team ethos is as hard an asset as any part of the machine. It's planned, structured, and maintained by a few time-tested elements that UnStoppable cultures always seem to share.

Graham Weston first learned those lessons at Fish Camp.

FISH CAMP

We've seen the power of culture shape success in every kind of organization, but there's no better example than Graham's exposure as a freshman to the legendary culture of the Texas A&M Aggies.

The Aggies are so cognizant of cultural power, they send every new freshman on a week's retreat before he or she ever sets foot on campus to learn how to act like an Aggie, talk like an Aggie, know tradition like an Aggie, sing songs around The Bonfire like an Aggie—in short, be a team member who belongs to the Aggies. For some reason, this weeklong orientation retreat is called Fish Camp. It's done in fun and in love but it's also taken very seriously. And the influence of Fish Camp has carried all the way through to the culture of belonging that embraces 5,000 employees at Rackspace.

Graham recounts the experience and explains what it has meant to him this way: "I went to a little rural high school, and I was never one of the popular, athletic kids who everyone wanted to invite everywhere and be with. I wasn't the last to be picked for sports—*I wasn't even picked!* The only guys not on the football team in high school were me and the goth guy. (I was on the Milk Judging team.)

"My parents weren't from America and so I didn't know about a lot of traditions, including applying to college. My high school chem teacher, a loyal Aggie, sat a small group of us who must've looked like we had some promise down one day and put an application in front of us. We just filled it out. It was the only college I knew about and the only place I applied.

"The first thing they did when we became new Aggies was send us all to orientation at Fish Camp. It was a revelation for me. It was the first time I was ever invited to join a winning team—in this case, a whole long tradition, a long line of greatness. They tell you the stories, the traditions, the songs, all the stuff you need to walk into freshman year as a member of the clan. Accelerated Aggie Proficiency training. 'Once an Aggie, Always an Aggie,' 'Highway 6 runs both ways,' 'Anything you do twice is a tradition,' 'Don't be a 2 percenter.' You learn about The Bonfire,[3] Aggie Muster, and Silver Taps.

"Suddenly, you belong to something really big, really important. A&M was masterful about building that sense of belonging. State schools were easy to get in and easy to flunk out of, but you definitely wanted to be one of the 50,000 who stayed.

"Looking back, it wasn't conscious at first but the culture we built at Rackspace is so obviously Aggie-inspired. The seeds are all over: Calling ourselves 'Rackers,' our traditions, belonging, being in a family. Rackers who get career offers from outside come to us saying things like, 'I just don't know if I'm ready to stop being a Racker.' The Aggies probably weren't thinking about it this way, but they were creating an incredible brand."

Isn't it fascinating to see how an amazing team-oriented culture in one institution (Texas A&M) can inspire a fantastic culture in a totally different and separate organization (Rackspace)? Like a beneficial virus, great cultures can spread their positive infection in unlikely and powerful directions.

BIG, SIMPLE CULTURAL SYMBOLS

If you want to build a culture of belonging that can support true teams, the ingredients are actually pretty basic. Just follow the example set at Texas A&M that transferred over to Rackspace.

Names and Language: Invent Your Own Names and Words

Names and words signify a common identity among members of anything. There's an insider's pride in knowing and using them. Everyone at Rackspace, from the chairman on down, is called a Racker. Not an associate, a rep, or an employee. A unique term that symbolizes membership in a unique organization.

---

[3]As described in Wikipedia, "The annual autumn event which symbolized Aggie students' 'burning desire to beat the hell outta T.U.,' a derogatory nickname for University of Texas at Austin." Now that's a famous college tradition.

"Racker" is just the start of the distinctive glossary of Rackspace. Graham Weston explains, "We have our own names for all kinds of things. To most people, a castle is a medieval fortress. To us, 'The Castle' is the converted mall in San Antonio that we've turned into an amazing global headquarters. We name traditions like our own version of Fish Camp, 'Rookie O' and 'Graduation.' We hold celebrations like 'Racktoberfest.' We don't give service, we give Fanatical Support. And to be asked to put on The Straightjacket in front of the whole company for actually providing Fanatical Support is one of the highest honors we can bestow. It's all part of our language and we're proud of every word of it."

Traditions: "Anything We Do Twice Is a Tradition"

The point is, traditions root cultures in ritual and continuity, and we humans love them. That's why great organizations like Rackspace are happy to err on the side of too many traditions any day. Putting every new Racker, from junior staff to managers through Rookie O is a tradition they experience right at the door. Taking the StrengthsFinder test and displaying the results, winning The Straightjacket, putting the Flags at their work stations, and the famous T-shirt wall, are other notable Rackspace traditions. The list goes on and on.

Visual IDs

There is a reason sports teams and armies wear uniforms. It's not just professional looking, it instantly identifies members of teams. Rackers aren't asked to wear uniforms, but the company employs consistent signage, logos, and visual cues, like the Racker name tags that show team members' personal strengths, as a way of visualizing reinforcing and emphasizing their unity and shared mission.

Big, Repeatable Cultural Values

It all comes down to the values the culture lives and dies by, not just the ones they talk about or hang as prints on a wall. Every member of the team must know those values, say them, and understand how decisions are guided by them every day. Remember, the greatest value- and mission-statements ever written are brief yet powerful— a small number of very important words. Some religious scholars have pointed out that the most important value statement in the Bible can fit on one line: "Do unto others as you'd have others do unto you."

The SEALs' values might be summarized like this:

> In battle individuals die, teams win: team is everything. We never quit, we are never out of the fight. We are all in, all the time. We will accomplish our mission.

At Rackspace, the company values are captured in just thirty words:

> Deliver fanatical support. Do the right thing always. Love our customers and believe in each other. Always manage to strengths, never fear. Leading Rackers is a privilege, not a right.

TRUE TEAMS AT RACKSPACE: THE UNTOLD STORY

Lorenzo Gomez has been a Racker from the earliest days of the company. We asked him to describe his experience of team at Rackspace, and the story he recounted was frankly remarkable:

"We were lucky enough to have set off the magic of true teams early on at Rackspace, and it became one of our greatest competitive advantages. It wasn't because we knew anything about the power of SEAL teams, true teams, or any of that at the time. What we had was (1) an existential threat to the company, (2) an entrepreneurial need to solve a problem, (3) we were all on the same mission, and (4) we tried a solution and, fortunately, it worked.

"The solution was to consolidate our service people into dedicated small teams for the first time. It was right after 9/11, when the economy went into a temporary tailspin and our smaller Internet-hosting customers were going out of business in droves. The churn turned into a hemorrhage. The customers that survived were the larger companies with more complex websites and service needs, but now there were a lot fewer to go around and they were demanding 24/7, high-touch service. We had to multiply our service levels overnight with the same staff and resources if we wanted to stay alive, let alone compete.

"We'd been operating as one big department, with Rackers working individually with clients on whatever problem was at hand. Whenever there was a bigger issue, they had to get up, walk to another area, and plead with an account person, a billing person, a tech person, or a business development person to help. All these specialties were needed at certain points to service larger customers. But the specialists had their own problems and their own managers to deal with. They weren't automatically willing or able to switch gears to help a junior account manager with another customer they'd never meet.

"And then a couple of entrepreneurial account leaders got together and had this 'what if?' moment. What if we put one Racker from each specialty into a bunch of self-contained units: small but complete teams that could handle any client problem? What if they physically sat within spitting distance of one another so they could collaborate by swiveling a chair or talking to the next desk? What if each team worked on a dedicated set of customers whose businesses and people they got to know like nobody's business? What if they all had skin in the game, so they all would share in the bonuses if they grew that customer's business or opened a new account?

"And here was the big game changer: what if each team actually ran itself like a mini-business, having P&L responsibility, tracking the sales revenues, the continuity, and the costs of each of its accounts so it could keep score?

"We tried it. It was amazing.

"Suddenly, everybody on each team was committed to the same goals and to solving the same problems together. The teams not only got to know their customers' issues, concerns, and businesses on a deep new level, they developed group expertise and a closeness that made them collaborate more smoothly and quickly as a team on every case. They started identifying with their teams and competing healthily for new business, bonuses, and better churn rates versus the other teams. Because they had P&L knowledge and accountability, they cared about the big picture and the little picture—profit, costs, and customer satisfaction, along with the need to fix the immediate problem.

"The amazing thing was that suddenly geeks, technical people, and billing people who'd never bothered and could just stay in the background—suddenly they were all selling! They were thinking about customers, proactively offering suggestions and solutions that would improve the customer's experience or expand an opportunity. We kept the size of the teams very small on purpose depending on the needs of each customer, but the basic rule was, 'No team bigger than one large pizza.'"

Customers loved the new teams. Rackers loved the new teams, too, because of the quantum leap it gave them in providing Fanatical Support. They loved the pride and camaraderie it built along the way.

The leaders of Rackspace didn't know it at the time, but they were carving their organization into a collection of true teams, not just nominal ones. They were giving each team important authority, responsibility with their accountability, a chance to be valued members of a winning unit, and a renewed, sharpened sense of inspiring mission where they depended on each other to avoid failure and reap the rewards. They were all in together, and it felt great.

Looking back on it now, Graham and other Rackers have come to recognize the similarity of their system of small powerful teams to the kind of teams the Navy SEALs rely upon. (They even occasionally refer to them in internal conversations as "our SEAL teams," while recognizing of course the enormous difference between the missions pursued by business-oriented teams and the literally life-and-death challenges that the heroic Navy SEALs undertake.)

What makes true teams *true* makes all the difference. The keen sense of mission, risk, mutual dependence, importance, and responsibility, all accepted together by teammates, unleashes the emotional mechanics that power it all. This requires cultural acceptance by the organization of one risk in particular—the risk of managing with lighter reins. In the case of Rackspace, that meant *trusting the teams* to track their own P&Ls like mini-businesses rather than having middle-management overseers, and allowing more entrepreneurial latitude in deed, not words.

But valued members on an inspiring mission will step up to it if you let them. What true teams can accomplish is a level of success not found any other way: true teams can be UnStoppable. Rackspace and the Navy SEALs show the way.

- A true team is an UnStoppable human force, your greatest multiplier. It motivates action and mitigates fear.
- Like a multi-cylinder engine compared to a single-cylinder one, the team's power is much greater than the sum of its parts.
- Teams leverage the deepest human instinct to belong to groups for collective power, production, and protection.
- True teams are different from nominal teams:
  - They function as a single organism, sharing the same mission.
  - The build on one another's strengths, never on fear or weakness.
  - Members "follow like leaders," knowing the big and little picture.
  - Authority shifts to specialists on demand.
  - They run on a clear, simple set of values.
  - They choose each other. Leaders who don't lead and members who won't sacrifice for others are ultimately rejected—no matter what higher authorities may decree.
- True teams exist only in cultures that venerate and support them.
- They use strong cultural symbols to reinforce identity—but cultures support them with acts and deeds first, words second.
- Those who understand team power are always on the lookout for potential teammates because they don't come along every day.
- As an Entrepreneur, never forget that the big question has two parts: "What's my idea?" and "Who's my team?" Both parts are equally important.

11

Everything You Need to Know about Succeeding with Customers (in about an Hour)

The customer . . . can fire everybody in the company from the chairman on down, simply by spending his money somewhere else.

—*Sam Walton*

MORE THAN ANY OTHER WORDS HANDED down by our founding fathers, there's one simple household saying, coined in America, that has changed the course of history and made our country the colossus of capitalism. It repositioned the ancient status quo that the elites and aristocrats were the only holders of power. It said that the vast, unwashed public that makes up the markets *matters*, that what's in other people's heads *matters*. Their free decisions on what to buy will decide who among us becomes the *next* barons and billionaires. The paradigm shifted from "we" on the inside to "they" on the outside. This magical phrase is:

The customer is always right.

It isn't in the Declaration of Independence or the U.S. Constitution, but it should have been. It's credited to one of the 19th-century entrepreneurs of retail like Marshall Field of Chicago or R. H. Macy, but no one knows for sure who first said. What we do know is that it's a MAP—a Master Aligning Principle that instantly sets the mission straight for any entrepreneur in any society where people are free to choose.

The customer is always right.

Well . . . almost.

TODAY THE SAYING NEEDS A TWEAK

The Internet age has disrupted a great many things, even the customer's privilege of always being right. Innovation is simply moving too fast for the customer to keep up. Humans demand trust, and trust takes time.

So while your new product may be technically superior, customers may continue to be wrong about it and not try it. Why? Because they've been burned by too many of your competitors' false claims before. It makes them suspicious until they see others happily using your product and decide they're ready to trust it. It means that this customer *isn't* right—until you teach her.

Your product may be so new, customers don't know they need it because they don't imagine it exists. Take the iPod and other famous Apple game changers. Steve Jobs and company took a risk and created a need the customer didn't know they had. Again, you have to show these customers and convince them. This is called sales.

So, here is the tweak the saying needs to be up to date, and you should need it 100 percent:

The customer may not always be right, but the customer always *decides*.

As the entrepreneur, you will have to take the risk. You will have to pursue the dream. You will have to build your team and develop the prototype and hold off the doubters.

But only customers will decide whether you're going to have a business. And you can't order them to do it. They must volunteer.

At this point it's worth defining . . .

WHAT'S A CUSTOMER?

A customer is someone who makes your business her number one choice to fill a need, is willing to give up money in return for your filling it, and does this again and again.

To be a customer, a person must:

1. Overcome *decision anxiety* and take *a risk* to try your business the first time—despite the risk that you may disappoint them and waste their time and money, causing pain, anger, frustration, and loss of opportunity.

2. Have their need fully satisfied as promised.

3. Trust you. People may buy from someone they don't necessarily like, but they will *not* buy from someone they don't trust.

4. Decide your business is the number one choice in your category—that is, that you continue to deliver the best value for the price they can afford.

5. Repeat. Buy from you again for all the above reasons. This may be the ultimate gating factor. A one-time trier who is unhappy with what you deliver is not a customer. He is a dissatisfied shopper, and if he tells anyone about you, he is guaranteed to be a detractor.

For your business to be a living, going concern, you must be able to attract and hold onto repeat customers. You must be recommendable by those happy customers to other potential customers.

Any business can open its doors, make false advertising claims, and get people to take a flyer once and never come back. Unless you cross the magic threshold—getting customers to buy you again after a trial—your enterprise will be nothing more than a fire that is quickly going out.

————

SUCCEEDING WITH CUSTOMERS

To succeed, you have to convert unattached civilians with no prior relationship into customers who will try, be satisfied, trust, choose, and
repeat. To do this, you must execute on all the mechanical requirements.
You need at least an MVP—a minimally workable prototype of a product that fills a customer's need. The product must provide a difference
that is superlative, important, believable, measurable, and own-able—
(a.k.a. a Dominant Selling Idea). In short, you need to execute on every
element of the UnStoppable Six to succeed with customers.

But recognizing the psychology of customers is critical, too,
because we're talking about emotions, loyalty, trust, fear, biases,
anxiety, and perceptions, after all—the most commonsense psychology there is. Generations of entrepreneurs have learned it from trial
and error, but mostly from the will to get it right because they knew
that only their customers would grant them success. That's exactly
how the founders of Rackspace learned it.

————

CUSTOMER PSYCHOLOGY

Nobody cares what you know until they know that you care.
—Famous Racker saying

All customers have needs, wants, fears, and pains like you and every
other human you know. So don't be surprised at how simple the
following direction is: the more you take away what customers don't
want and give them what they do want, the more you will succeed
with them. Here are the known issues no successful business must ever
ignore:

All Customers Hate Risk. Take It Away.

If you think because you are an entrepreneur and business owner you
are the only one who takes risk and needs to mitigate it, you haven't
been listening. Put yourself in your customers' shoes even for a

second and you'll see they're sailing on a sea of risk, just like you are. They take a risk every time they try a new product like yours—a risk that it won't work, that they'll be humiliated, that they'll lose time and money or the respect of their peers—or even get fired. The risk causes anxiety and pain in all prospects.

You job is to take that risk away.

Think I'm exaggerating the risks that customers face? Think again. Even though a particular purchase may seem relatively small, in your customer's world at the moment of decision, it can seem huge. A young woman who makes $400 a week in wages and decides to try a new shampoo not only risks throwing away her $16.95 but risks having a bad hair day for her hot date that night. For her, a bottle of shampoo is mission-critical.

The manager of a tech start-up choosing a cloud hosting company is just as concerned. If the company site goes down, if the customer support sucks, if there are hidden costs and fees, the start-up can lose its business before it has the chance to switch cloud vendors.

As a branding consultant, I knew and appreciated that when a customer finally picked my firm over all the others, often committing a major amount of their budget and only having one shot to get the solution right before a big deadline. Their jobs were on the line if we screwed up. My team knew we had a big personal responsibility as well as a professional one to those folks, and we acted that way.

So if you want to succeed with customers, find specific, actionable ways to take away the buyer's risk. This is why the smart sellers who invented modern retail created the money-back guarantee. That's why performing as promised counts so much. It's also why reputation and customer referrals matter to every business. They eliminate the perception of risk and evaporate the buyer's anxiety.

All Customers Have Pain. Take It Away.

A famous ad man of the *Mad Men* era was asked by a young social media marketer, "What is your philosophy of advertising that has made you so successful?" The ad man replied, "People have a headache. They want it to go away."

This is why performing as well or even better than the customer expects you to is an all-essential ingredient of success. People love whoever it is that solves a problem or fills a real need. Put all your energy and focus on understanding the exact nature and depth of your customer's problem, then on fixing it in a way that's obvious and true. Do it time after time and you will build trust, a base of repeat customers, and the referrals they bring.

All Customers Want You to Make Their Life Better. Do It.

Taking away the pain of a headache, the embarrassment of frizzy hair, or a difficult, costly production bottleneck makes a customer's life better. So does bringing them a new pleasure or delight, like putting 10,000 songs in the palm of their hand with an iPod or delivering a really wonderful, relaxing Caribbean cruise.

In fact, this is the ultimate answer to the eternal business question: "Why do I need it? Why does the world need you to be in business at all?"

The answer is to make lives better by making people happier, healthier, smarter, more free of pain and fear, sexier, and more appealing. It doesn't have to be a big thing—remember the 1 percent rule—just a better thing.

This again, is about performance. This is what you must be number one in. Make sure it's obvious to the eye and consistent to the touch.

All Customers Want to Feel That Their Problem Is Your Problem

Customers are obsessed with one set of problems in the world—their own—and they have an absolute right to be that way. And they expect you to share their obsession. They don't simply want you to make them feel important, they want to feel like they're *your one and only*—kind of like a jealous boyfriend or girlfriend.

Don't underestimate this dynamic. You must show customers you care about the little things and the big things, the things that say you're listening and making them your highest priority. This eases their anxiety and generates trust. Action is always what counts, but the right words and attention matter, too. Just don't ever skimp on the action.

All Customers Want It Easier

You product needs to be easy to buy, easy to install, easy to understand, easy to afford, easy to use, easier than your competition's, and easier than the customer expected. It's a universal law that easy beats hard and simple beats complicated. Your customer's world is encumbered enough by the tangle of modern life and business. No one ever lost a customer for making it too easy.

Great salespeople have known this for centuries. That's why you'll see them taking away all the obstacles that get in the way of purchase. A customer may be sold on your solution, but if there are too many forms to fill out, too many hoops to jump through, too long a wait for delivery, or too many options to choose from, they'll give up in frustration and seldom come back. On the other hand, if all your competitors make them jump through hoops that you can streamline into one-stop shopping and one-click ordering, you'll win the business on that difference alone (providing of course that your product performance is up to par).

All Customers Want It Faster—But Not Too Fast. Doing It Right Matters Most.

A successful entrepreneur once said, "Speed is never wasted." Amen. There has never been a customer who had a problem that didn't want it fixed fast. If you are in a customer-service–oriented business, fast is always your friend. Just be careful not to be so fast that the job isn't done right or the product won't perform. Over time, you'll learn that "doing it right the first time" is most important to most customers. So faster is always better—as long as you fully perform.

All Customers Want Proof. Make Sure They See It.

This one is critical for getting prospective customers to give you that first order, and for longtime customers to stay loyal to you and your brand. Unfortunately, "you're only as good as your last performance" is a fact of life for most businesses that aren't monopolies or public utilities. Customer loyalty only goes so far. When you go to your favorite restaurant, you expect to get a great meal with minor variance. After all, that meal is still pretty expensive for most folks. A loyal customer will cut you some slack when you fall down once, maybe twice. But that's about it. Budgets and time are too precious in today's world. If you fail to perform, they may still like you but they can't afford to stay with you.

Here's one of my all-time favorite proof stories:

Once the founders of Rackspace decided they were going to become the world's number one customer support company in a category that offered none, and in a market made cynical by too many false claims, they had to prove it. They came up with signature language to flag their position (Fanatical Support), but then they needed signature deeds and behavior to make it tangible as well.

So they changed their system so that any support call would always be picked up by a human being, never a recording. They staffed up so calls could be answered on the first ring and every customer could be assigned a dedicated team. They made sure all Rackers knew they were empowered to do whatever it took to solve a customer problem—that no one would ever be reprimanded for going the extra mile and using extra resources, as long as it was to serve the customer. Then they even challenged their own people to test it and believe it for themselves.

Graham Weston recounts what happened next: "One of our early salespeople was trying to close what would've been by far our biggest customer ever—the order would've been for 22 servers. Unheard of. The salesperson got on the phone and said to the prospect, 'You say support is important? Well, we're going to give you Fanatical Support. Here's what that means. When you have a problem, our team will be there with you until it's fixed—24/7, 365 days a year. That means, if you call us up at 2 AM on Christmas Eve with a question about Linux, our team will be there, just like if you called right now. Go ahead and test us—we're serious.'

"Sure enough, the prospect actually called back at 2 AM on Christmas Eve. They got a Racker on one ring. They asked a Linux question. The Racker said brightly, 'Sure, let's get right on that.

I'm going to bring some other members of my team on the line, Lorenzo and Debbie, who have more Linux expertise than me and can answer it for you.'

"The prospect said, 'Thanks, Merry Christmas,' hung up the phone, and ordered 22 servers.

"We said it, we proved it. We succeeded with that customer."

More important, they made sure they were prepared to do the same thing for thousands of other customers—and to do it over and over again, proving their performance unceasingly.

We think that's a pretty good definition of UnStoppable.

THE MOST IMPORTANT PRINCIPLE OF ALL: WEAR YOUR VALUES ON YOUR SLEEVE

The psychology behind your customers' feelings about you depends entirely on the psychology of your own people—your teammates, partners, associates, every stakeholder who serves them; the ones who want to believe they are valued members of a winning team on an inspiring mission. If they believe their mission is to succeed with customers above all else, they will do everything in their power to help their team accomplish it. When they believe, they make customers believe. It's one closed circuit. Customers want to believe they can trust you to solve a problem and enhance an opportunity. Actions prove it.

Your people work the same way. Values need to be articulated clearly, simply, and repeatably with a few words. Then, only the actions of leaders walking the walk will prove your priorities and make them real.

For Rackspace to become the Fanatical Support company, company leaders had to allow their simple values to become real with Rackers. If they said no one would be reprimanded for doing the right thing for a customer, they had to mean it. If they said they were going to answer the phone on one ring, they had to invest the resources and incur the extra cost to do it. They had to live their values and their mission inside to make it real to the people who would bring it to life on the outside.

"Character is what you do when nobody else is looking," but people are *always* looking to see that we mean what we say. Your values are paramount because they always are in any culture that puts customers first.

What's Measured Is What Matters—The Net Promoter Score®

Finally, if something matters in a company or a culture, and you want to prove that it does, then you must measure it, for two reasons:

1. Because keeping score is the only way to know whether you're going forward, backward, or nowhere, and
2. Because when you care enough to measure a quantity and report on it, you're telling everyone in the culture that the subject really matters.

Nothing mattered more to Rackspace than their mission to be the best service organization in the business—and for the market to know it, too. They knew this reputation only counted in other people's heads, not their own, so they needed a way to measure it. And after a few years of searching, they discovered the Net Promoter Score (NPS)—a system of measuring customer happiness first introduced by Fred Reichheld in 2003 in a *Harvard Business Review* article titled "The One Number You Need to Grow."[1] They've used it as a key customer retention asset worldwide, ever since.

The NPS says that the ultimate measure of how you're doing with customers can be answered by a single question after using your product: "Would you recommend us to a friend?" One could say that this question is the single most important and powerful question in customer loyalty. If the answer is yes, you've not only succeeded with that customer, but with the others she'll inevitably urge to try

---

[1] Frederick F. Reichheld, "The One Number You Need to Grow," *Harvard Business Review*, December 2003, http://hbr.org/2003/12/the-one-number-you-need-to-grow/ar/1.

your product. It's more important today than ever in our digital word-of-mouth age where customers can promote you or dis you with a touch of the screen.

Graham Weston reports, "The NPS was revolutionary for us because it was so simple and it actually worked with our people and customers." It rates whether a customer would recommend you on a low-to-high scale of 1–10, and it doesn't allow cheating. Customers who pick a score from 1 to 6 are actually called "detractors." They are unhappy with their experience and they will broadcast it to others. Those who pick 7 to 8 are "passive," neither here nor there. Only customers who score you as a 9 to 10 on whether they'd recommend you are your promoters. They are delighted with your service. They will actively tell others because people love to tell their friends and colleagues about experiences they love—almost as much as they complain when an experience is bad. Either way, they will do it.

Because the test is so simple—unlike those 25-minute surveys the airlines ask you to take after they've already kept you on hold for an hour—a high percentage of people will stop what they're doing to answer you. And once you've broken the ice and gotten permission to ask this simple question, they'll give you an additional golden opportunity.

You get to ask them, "Why?"

The "verbatims" you get are worth their weight in gold. You add up all the scores and get one numerical value that you can track to see how you're doing over time.

By now, you should see a basic UnStoppable theme at work in the Net Promoter Score. NPS is not 100 percent perfect, but it represents one of the best aspects of the UnStoppable doctrine: simple, consolidated truth. It's another MAP—one magic question that automatically lines up a series of critical answers in the right sequence and guides you in the right direction with a single ask.

Think about it: to answer 9 to 10 on the recommend-to-a-friend scale, the customer has to trust you, be willing to buy again from you, think you're worth the price, imply that you're a number one choice, and have a positive enough emotional impression of your people and product that she's willing to tell other people what she respects about you.

It also helps you avoid the "too much data makes you dumber" trap. As we've seen, the biggest mistake in research, often attempted by Optimizers for efficiency reasons, is to ask too many questions on too many subjects when they get the chance to talk to a customer. The questions start to contaminate one another, the respondents and clients get confused, and the research yields a mishmash of nothing. Less is more when it comes to meaningful customer research.

Instead, ask a much smaller number of much more important questions. The NPS asks just one ("Would you recommend us to a friend or colleague?"), and only one more ("Why?") if granted permission.

The NPS has allowed Rackspace to measure how they're succeeding with our customers—to pat themselves on the back when they improve and smack themselves on the backside when they don't. Some legendary customer-centric organization in other industries use it as well, including Zappos.com (the online shoe seller) and Nordstrom.

The Psychology of Your Customers

We talked about what all customers and team members want in order for you to succeed with them. Now there is only one group left to mention: *your* customers, the ones in your category, your geography, your affinity group.

You find out the deepest details about what they need, want, like, and don't like, and how they want to be treated, sold, and serviced, by doing one thing: asking them.

You must go outside and talk to them. This is the simplest, most important advice you can take from *The UnStoppables*. Your customers want to be listened to and cared for. If they believe you do these things, they'll give you the keys to succeeding with them.

Those are the keys that count.

- The customer isn't always right but *always* decides.
- A customer is someone who makes you their number one choice and pays you for it.
- To succeed with customers:
  - Know they hate risk. Take it away.
  - Know they have pain. Take it away.
  - Make their life better in an obvious way
  - Make their problem your problem.
  - Make it easier.
  - Make it faster—but not so fast it's not done right.
  - Give them proof.
  - Show them your values and that you live them with your team.
  - Remember: "What's measured is what matters."
  - Go outside and ask them if they would recommend your business . . . and why.

12

Everything You Need to Know about Making Yourself Famous (in about an Hour)

TO BE A BUSINESS, YOU HAVE to have customers. To get customers, they have to know about you. What they know has to make them want to buy.

It's that simple.

This is what we mean by making yourself famous. We mean getting seen and heard in your marketplace—whether it's the local community or a global one—standing for an idea of value, and being talked about by others. If you do this, you'll end up with a name that has a specific reputation attached, commonly known as a *brand*.

When you discover what your brand is, you'll know that it will always be the center of what makes and keeps you famous. That's why it's the focus of this chapter. Along with True Teams, crafting a unique *selling* brand is one of the biggest multipliers of entrepreneurial success, and it's doable by anyone who takes a few simple steps to find a great selling brand and control it.

All your marketing and sales communications should beat from the same heart: one strong brand foundation, the one big selling idea that sets you apart. The process that comes later on—advertising, free media, events, and PR—is more tactical and technical. It can be read about, learned in classrooms, or hired.

Every business can use the following brand tools for free to help make themselves famous. They've been honed for decades by brand titans who put these principles to the test, turning tiny start-ups into global giants. The power behind your brand will always be your Unique Difference—what we've already termed a DSI, the first key element in the Strategic Three. You'll find that most of the rules that apply to differences and brands are identical because their essential mission is the same: to set you apart in the fastest, most memorable way.

No advice we can give you is more important than this: As a leader, you have to think about your brand and the Unique Difference behind it from day one—and every day you show up for work thereafter. Think of it this way: Your brand is just your *Unique Difference*, turned into *your reputation*.

Understanding how this works is essential.

CAUTION: FAMOUS WORKS BOTH WAYS

The world is full of awesome products that no one has ever heard of because they are sitting on a bench in an inventor's garage. The inventor did nothing to make them famous. It's also full of not-the-best-but-good-enough products that have made entrepreneurs hugely successful because those entrepreneurs *were* the best at telling others about their products, getting famous in their markets, getting distribution, and becoming the standard that everybody bought.

The world is also full of people, places, and things that are universally famous but that no one would buy or buy from in a million years because they represent something terrible. Every American adult and child knows about Bernie Madoff and Lance Armstrong, but we wouldn't elect either one president. You must be famous for value and trust—good things, not bad—if you want someone to buy from you and if you want to become a *selling brand*.

The entrepreneur's job is thus to execute not only on a prototype-building plan, but also on a fame-building plan.

BRANDING 101

It's Not Optional

Picture this scene:[1] You walk into a party. There's a woman in a police uniform, a young man with blue spiked hair, and three other people in casual clothes. Okay, so there's a female cop and a punked-out computer geek. Who are the other three? The hostess comes over. "Let me introduce you to Dr. Harwood, head of neurosurgery at Stanford; Bob Boyd, the attorney who just won the big class action case against wearing your pants down around your ass in public; and my friend, Bob." Based on his nerdy-looking eyeglasses, you figure Bob is an accountant. Then you see his diamond-accented Rolex. Bob moves up to hedge fund guy.

Between the uniforms, your hostess, and your preconceived notions, you've just judged, valued, and categorized—in other words, branded—six people in 15 seconds. And guess what?— They've just branded you.

We don't think about it, we just do it. We're wired that way. It's our single-minded caveman urge to simplify.

The fact is, we can't *not* form these instantaneous brand impressions. We can't *not* make these judgments. Our primitive brains want us to form snap judgments on the least amount of information, so they give us automatic mental rules of thumb to help us do it, like "The one I know is the one that's safe," and "Familiar is better."

---

[1] Scene courtesy of Bill Schley and Carl Nichols Jr., *Why Johnny Can't Brand: Rediscovering the Lost Art of the Big Idea* (Kindle edition, 2010).

The human proclivity for snap judgments means that if you're going to have a business, branding is not optional. The only choice you have is to shape your brand and control it yourself. Otherwise, your customers and competitors will do it for you. And you won't like the tagline when they do.[2]

Brands are more important than ever these days, for two reasons. First, because there used to be just one kind of everything— one kind of soup, one kind of soap—but now there are 350,000 stock-keeping units (SKUs) at the supermarket. We need help telling them apart.

Second, we live in a digital word-of-mouth age in which every customer can broadcast impressions and likes or dislikes to a thousand friends in a second. UnStoppable marketers develop brands that are distinctive from others so that customers will talk about them in colorful (and positive) ways.

What Kind of Brand Must You Be?

If a brand is your name attached to a specific reputation in the customer's mind, then Wheaties, BMW, Red Bull, and the NFL are all brands. But so are North Korea and Al Qaeda. They're just not positive ones. They are names attached to reputations that most of us find repellent. We wouldn't buy them—but they're brands just the same.

The only kind of brand we want is a *selling brand:* a name attached to an idea that's a powerful reason to buy.

Entrepreneurs must build their brands on a Unique Difference that has the five elements that make it a DSI—elements that are always worth repeating. It's a difference that's:

Superlative—says we're number one, the best at something

Important—what we're best in really matters to the customer

Believable—it makes sense coming from us

---

[2]Ibid.

Measurable—we make the difference obvious; it can be seen and felt

Own-able—it is uniquely available from us; a difference only we give you

A DSI is at the center of all great and famous brands. It's the one big idea you want to stand for above all others in the customer's mind—the "one idea" as you'll recall from the One Item of Carry-on Rule. Make sure your brand can stand up to the DSI test. Here are some examples of brands known around the world because they do:

Volvo is the safest car

Toyota is the most reliable car

Ferrari is the world's most famous sports car

Hertz stands for the biggest rental car company

Enterprise is the rental car company that picks you up

Nike is the shoe more pro athletes wear

Apple makes the most stylish high-tech gadgets

Nordstrom provides the world's best customer service in retail

Rackspace provides the world's best customer service in the cloud

The one, the only, the biggest, the best—these brands are all DSIs in their categories. What makes you the number one choice every day? What do you give the customer that nobody else does? What's the one biggest advantage that would make people buy if they knew about it? What sets you apart in your market area? Why the heck are you here?

Find and nail this idea. If you can't, you need to adjust your product, your business model, your market, or your mission until you do.

Notice we did *not* say to adjust your *words*. If you don't have an idea of the distinct value that you deliver, your brand is worthless and no amount of slick words can help. Brands are not made from words, only suggested by them. Brands are made from promises kept and real performance—what you do in return for the customer's money and trust, over and over again.

When you figure out what your DSI is and find a way to deliver it reliably over and over again, then by all means put that in the words and use the tools that help you get famous, faster. Use nothing but UnStoppable language whenever you can—language that is specific, vivid, concise, and story-centered. Just don't forget the classic advertising principle: "Great advertising for a lousy product just makes it die faster."

How to Brand: Name It, Frame It, and Claim It

Name It   If you can dream it, then name it.

A great politician once said, when asked why he remembered so many voters' names, "The sweetest sound to any man's ears is the sound of his own name." Names are the first words we learn and say. Even a pet parakeet can learn its own name. Likewise, there is no more powerful branding and getting-famous tool than a great name.

This is why the movie studios took a charming young actor named Archie Leach and turned him into Cary Grant—and why little Ralphie Lifshitz from the Bronx gave himself a name tweak to become Ralph Lauren. What's in a name? Everything.

The greatest names are (1) easy to say, (2) colorful or descriptive, and (3) *set up your DSI*. In fact, they launch your selling idea in the minds of customers every time they are heard or seen. Every time they are uttered, *a unique reason to buy comes right along with it*. A great name is the branding gift that keeps on giving!

Whenever possible, give yourself a descriptive name in real words. One of our new all-time favorites is 5-hour ENERGY, the liquid energy shot found on the counter of every convenience store in America. (Yes, the name is printed just like that, capital letters and all, on every product label and in every advertisement.) It's like an elevator pitch in three words, describing precisely what the customer will get every time he or she buys and downs a bottle of the stuff.

Other great examples include Diehard Batteries, Invisible Fence, Facebook, Head & Shoulders shampoo, LinkedIn, 3 Day Startup, and Air Blade hand dryers.

Budget car rental, Sleep Eze, StairMaster, FOCUS Factor memory pills, Krazy Glue, Roach Motel, 8 Minute Abs, and Omaha Steaks. In each case the name captures the product's DSI and thereby starts the selling process immediately.

Because so many dictionary words are already reserved as names and websites these days, you can often make up descriptive-sounding names by combining them. The best are the ones where the derivative words are pretty obvious to anyone: Groupon (group + coupon), Jumbotron, Netflix, CarMax, Wikipedia (wiki + encyclopedia), Duracell, Entelligence, and Compaq (which started out by making the first compact, portable personal computer).

Other great names may violate the above rules but work nonetheless because they are fun to say, easy to remember, and slide off the tongue. If they perform and become popular with customers, they become new words all by themselves, like Swiffer, Google, and Twitter. Amazon is another great example. The name says nothing about what they do. They succeeded because they were a monopoly in a brand-new category. Their colorful name eventually became its own descriptive word and a category.

Most entrepreneurs can't afford to take that kind of gamble. Why would you name your energy drink Bambaloosie when you could call it 5-hour ENERGY—a name that customers hear and think, "Hey, I want that!" If at all possible, avoid saddling yourself with a name that's inherently meaningless—empty initials like GRX Inc., or a nonsense name like iFloozient. A name like that is simply a wasted opportunity. You're opting to start from a brand hole: no one has any idea what you do or why they should care. Then you have to teach them from scratch.

The best entrepreneurs have an instinctive urge to name their business as soon as they've got an exciting idea, because that's the first step to making an idea more tangible and visible in their own minds, let alone in the minds of others. A movie producer's first question always is: what's it called? They know that an evocative title like *Animal House, Star Wars, Raiders of the Lost Ark*, or *Back to the Future* excites the senses and launches the whole pitch in the right direction. A generic movie name like *Playing for Keeps, People Like Us, The Day*, or *Any Day Now* (all real movies that were released in 2012 and promptly forgotten) just allows you to be invisible.

Brand Names Galvanize the Troops and Focus Your Mission   We never stop being impressed as we see this effect happen again and again: just coming up with a good, sharp, or provocative brand name works like magic to fire up and refocus founders and followers.

A friend of ours was retiring from the Navy and starting up a handyman services business backed by a do-it-yourself website. He was hoping to systematize, grow, and eventually replicate the business through myriad local franchises. He had come a long way, but still didn't have a name that excited him—one that would really click with customers. Every form of "Mr. Handyman Do-It-Yourself" was taken. We applied naming principle number one: build on your unique selling idea. His was: Count on us to get there fast, and fix it for the fairest price, always.

We came up with Fixit Express. Boom! It launched his proposition, and even set up taglines like "Fix it for less with Fixit Express." It was like lighting a fuse for this founder and his team. They created a new logo and graphics for their trucks, and started selling with new confidence and excitement.

Graham Weston and his colleagues at Rackspace have seen the same magic happen when naming everything from the new open-source cloud operating system called OpenStack ("The Operating System of the Open Cloud") to San Antonio's first 24/7 collaborative workspace for innovators and entrepreneurs, Geekdom.

And just in case you still don't think names are important, there's this classic naming story. A few years ago, fresh ocean fish from New England's legendary Grand Banks was getting scarcer and more expensive. So some South American entrepreneurs discovered they could farm-raise an incredible, edible white fish that would be a hit in the American market. Its meat was mild, firm, and flavorful, perfect for restaurant chefs to work with. It was plentiful and inexpensive. And it had one horrible problem.

It was called the *Patagonian toothfish*. Food preferences are famously subjective and psychological. A Patagonian toothfish sounded like something boney, sharp-fanged, and ugly, right out of a nightmare. You didn't want to be in the same room with a toothfish, let alone eat one. Compared to elegantly named species like salmon, branzino, tilapia, and mahi-mahi, its popularity was nil.

Until someone simply changed the name.

The new name was *Chilean sea bass*.

How charming, a fish with real class. Hadn't we already been eating that one for years? Chilean sea bass became a restaurant staple overnight. We won't tell anyone.

This name did something especially powerful—it *reframed* the whole idea, from an ugly, toothy derelict from a sketchy place to an Ivy League graduate—a sea bass—from the lovely, exotic nation of Chile. It was a new name and a new frame at the same time.

Framing is the next bit of branding magic you can do to make yourself famous faster and more consistently. What works for Chilean sea bass works for just about anything.

Frame It

You've heard of political candidates putting a "spin" on an issue, also known as "defining the opponent's identity with voters," or marketers creating a "position" for their brands. They're all doing the same thing: *framing*. Framing is simply helping others to think about an idea, a product, or a person in the positive way you want them to, so they form an impression and attach a value that advances your cause. If you frame a product or business right, you control what people think about your brand. And you always frame around your DSI—the idea that makes your business the number one choice.

The Simplest Way to Frame: Give Them a Box to Put You in Customers instinctively form an impression of us whether we ask them to or not, then they file us in a mental box that occupies a unique place in the brain. Once you're in that box, it's very hard to get out of it.

So the simplest and most direct way of framing is to *give them the box* to put you in. That is, declare in the fewest, most specific, and most vivid terms the answer to the most basic buying questions.

First, tell them in what area you are the number one choice.

Second, if it's not already obvious or implied (because you're a new kind of product, like a Swiffer), tell them the best thing you do to make their life better—that is, what problem you solve or new opportunity you bring.

For example, "We are the number one choice because we are . . ."

Texas' most popular BBQ

The one four out of five dentists recommend

America's number one roofing specialist

The only shoes that breathe

Milk's favorite cookie

Canada's most experienced Lasik surgeons

The only salt that won't clump

The fastest outboards

The most unbreakable trash bags

The 99 percent on-time airline

The operating system of the open cloud

Every one of the above statements tells the customer unmistakably what you do, that you are best in it, and why they should care. That's a lot of information for any seller to give a buyer in an instant, and is an excellent starting frame.

It is remarkable how many good companies fail to give customers any kind of frame at all to start with. They leave us wondering about what they do and why, forcing us to make it up on their own. How many websites do you see where you have no idea what they are selling or what they are expert in until you dig into the third paragraph of "About Us"? How many TV commercials seem to keep the product a mystery until the last two seconds, baffling us and wasting our time by selling us nothing?

Giving customers a frame that tells them immediately what you're offering will put you ahead of the majority of your competitors, and well on your way to getting famous.

The Only Way to Change a Mind: Replace the Box   Many products fall into categories where there is already an established leader and a big general frame that customers put them in. In these cases you need to *reframe*—essentially replace the old box with a new one—just like we did with fear in Chapter 4. As we saw, the universal frame for fear is that it's bad, painful, and must be avoided. But the SEALs taught us that the trick is to reframe it:

> Fear is your friend. Fear gives you a winning edge. Don't fear it, *steer* it.

When you hear the common expression "think outside the box," it essentially means replacing an old frame with a new one. Reframing takes something we thought we knew and shows us how it's really something else. It gives us a whole new box to replace the old one. And it doesn't ask us to come up with the new box ourselves, it just hands it to us.

For instance, a Snickers Bar is traditionally framed as candy. And candy for most of us is framed as frivolous, forbidden food that makes you fat and rots your teeth. To get us to think outside the box about a candy bar, the Snickers people were smart enough to furnish a nifty new frame: "Snickers is packed with peanuts so it really satisfies." In other words, "Don't think of Snickers as candy, think of it as a nutritious snack." Millions of people who wanted permission to eat a candy bar suddenly got it and they gratefully snapped up this new frame. Snickers sales soared.

Likewise with Guinness. Beer is framed as an alcoholic beverage, an historic vice far more serious than candy bars. But Guinness famously changed the frame. What you didn't know, they said, is that "Guinness is good for you." Then they told you the story about all the vitamins and minerals in it, and how it's the only brew in the world served in hospitals (in Dublin, of course). Having another Guinness was no longer just another irresponsible indulgence. Guinness was good food. Eat up!

Once an idea is framed in our heads, it is *very* hard to dislodge. We love the frames we've already got, which makes thinking outside the box extremely difficult. That's why we entrepreneurs must replace our customers' old mental boxes if we're ever going to get them to try our new product and tell others about it. And that's why the reframing technique is so important for innovators and entrepreneurs and why it's done every day.

Framing the Easy Way—with Simple Metaphors   Specific metaphors are the framer's power tool. A metaphor creates a word picture in the mind. It says that one thing—often something familiar—is just like something else. As a result, it can deliver a surprising twist:

A problem is just an opportunity in work clothes.

Pork is the other white meat.

He ain't heavy, he's my brother.

The car snowplow drivers take to work.

The thinking man's cigarette.

Failing is learning.

No food tastes as good as skinny feels.

Mints so strong they come in a metal box.

Sharing is caring.

It's like having 10,000 songs in your pocket.

It's not just a cell phone, it's a computer.

It's not TV, it's HBO.

It's the soup that eats like a meal.

Framing with Famous Comparisons   This is such a simple and effective reframing trick that it's worth a special mention. If you can compare your unknown product to something already liked, trusted, and famous, you'll get an instant trusted frame every time.

Q: What's LinkedIn?
A: It's Facebook for business people.

Q: What's OpenStack?
A: It's Linux for the cloud.

Q: What software are you building?
A: It's Microsoft Office on a smart phone.

Claim It

Once you've figured out your DSI and framed it effectively, you've got to launch it into the marketplace. You've got to speak up and have people hear you. You've got to put it into a claim that you can shout, sing, text, or otherwise have people repeat to make you famous for one consistent, positive selling idea.

A claim is your sales proposition put into words: "Use this product, get this unique benefit." It's an invitation to think about your brand the way you want customers to if they will simply try it.

What you claim is what you want to become famous for. It's a call to the customer to pay attention and realize you're here to solve their problem better than anyone else. Only make claims you can prove with performance. You can make the most dramatic, provocative, challenging claims to get the most attention *as long as* you pay them off with performance.

A claim that doesn't come true is an empty claim. Such a claim that misleads your customers with advertising speak, that sugar-coats but has no real substance (like "Quality, selection, and price!") is called puffery. If you are going to step out of the batter's box the way Babe Ruth did and point beyond the center field fence, you better hit the next pitch out of the park. The fans will then tell your story and make you famous. Unfortunately, they'll also tell it if you whiff.

The Best Kinds of Claims   The best kinds of claims are specific, dramatic, and challenging, stated in the fewest number of words that people can easily repeat to others. That means a claim put into a Micro-Script will almost always bring your highest yield because people are more likely to talk about it, tweet it, or text it. There is no better way to become famous than to have other people talk about you via word of mouth—not just because it's free, but because it derives trust from a customer's accepted source, a friend or a peer. Nothing is more important for your success than establishing trust in everything you do.

We defined a Micro-Script earlier as short phrase that tells a story in a way that people like to remember or repeat. Micro-Scripts almost always contain a metaphor, often have rhythm or rhyme in the language, and are specific and descriptive. Look again at the examples of famous phrases and taglines we listed above. Virtually every one is written as a Micro-Script.

Having a Great Tagline   After brand names, taglines are the second most powerful branding element—when you follow the rules that make them right. That means they are written as Micro-Scripts, they are specific, and they advance one idea—your Dominant Selling Idea. Empty strings of sugary fluff like "A Passion for Excellence" and "Driven to Perform," which tell us nothing and could be stamped on any package, are not what we mean. We mean taglines written in UnStoppable Language: specific, visual, brief, easy to remember, and repetitive, like:

Milk chocolate that melts in your mouth, not in your hand.

A diamond is forever.

We only make one kind of car: The Ultimate Driving Machine

A big burst of fruit in every bite.

The few, the proud, the Marines.

The Quicker Picker Upper.

My opponent is a flip-flopper.

Great taste, less filling.

Kills the weeds, not the lawn.

Name, Frame, and Claim—All in One

By now, you may have noticed that these keys to making your-self famous often overlap because they're all working toward the same goal: to plant your DSI in the customer's mind. The more you make these branding tools support and reinforce one another, the more powerful they'll be in making you famous. The framing lines we listed a few pages back are often great claims as well, used in famous taglines. The great names we cited, like Diehard batteries and Invisible Fence, also give you the frame and imply the claim all in one.

In fact, if you combine a great name and a tagline that both frame and claim at the same time, you'll have the most powerful brand and fame-building tool there is—a one-line elevator pitch that the customer repeats, every time she says it!

Cialis: The only 36-hour ED pill

Diehard Batteries: Never get stuck again

Splenda: The no-calorie sweetener made from sugar so it tastes like sugar

Sinners and Saints Restaurant: Food for your mood

Las Vegas Convention and Visitors Authority: What happens in Vegas, stays in Vegas

Chobani Greek Yogurt: Twice the protein, half the fat of regular yogurt

THE FOUR-LINE ELEVATOR PITCH

If you can describe your company or product in about four succinct lines, your pitch will be worth its weight in gold, because not only can you and all your people remember it, all your customers can, too. You'll be ahead of 90 percent of your competitors who can't succinctly explain what they do. Here's a pitch for a product we named a few years ago called Home ATM:

- It's called Home ATM;
- It's home banking on your computer that works just like an ATM;
- It's so easy to use, like an ATM, it doesn't need a manual; and
- Eight top banks have found they can now have an ATM in every home.

The four-line elevator pitch answers these questions for the customer: What's it called? What does it do? Why do I need it? Why should I believe you?

The four-line elevator pitch is a favorite of the world's best salespeople, and we'll talk about it some more in our next chapter.

———

HOW NAME, FRAME, AND CLAIM MADE RACKSPACE A MULTIBILLION-DOLLAR COMPANY

It took a host of factors to enable Rackspace to rise from nowhere to overtake its early competitors and grow to its current market-leading status. But none was more important than its founders' decision to think about the unique difference they would stand for, and how they could build a selling brand from that difference, starting on day one.

They started with a good descriptive name. In those days, computer servers were lined up in metal racks. Indeed, the company's business was to sell its customers "rack space" on their professionally configured, maintained, and secure racks.

So the name Rackspace described "what" their service was, but it didn't say "why" a customer should make them their number one choice. It wasn't a unique frame for a DSI that customers could use to set them apart in the category—especially since, in 1998, there were lots of competitors offering a similar "what."

Fortunately, the Rackspace team made defining the ultimate "why" a big priority, even traveling *en masse* to meet Jack Trout, the renowned positioning expert. They experimented with a range of DSIs until they found the difference their customers were desperate to have—the best 24/7 service and support the industry had ever seen. They framed it as so awesome and extreme, it was Fanatical Support. They told customers, "This is the only thing we make, the only thing we do, and the only thing you'll get, whether you have one server or 10,000."

The frame, worded as a Micro-Script, helped Rackspace get famous on the outside. But just as important, it made them feel famous *on the inside*. As Graham Weston explains, "Once we came up with the phrase Fanatical Service, we had a rallying cry, a set of words to stand for, an identity that every teammate could be a part of. Every Racker could tell you in two words what our mission was and why we came to work every single day: we were here to bring our customers Fanatical Support and all the good things it implied."

Graham adds, "Everything we did over the next 10 years arose from that single core. The best thing we did after finding that two-word phrase was to *stick with it*—not change it every time a new marketing director came on board like so many companies do—so it could grow from a seedling into a big oak tree. In the process, it helped make us famous, all as a natural outgrowth of doing what we do best for our customers."

If you dream of creating your own multibillion-dollar empire, follow the example of Rackspace. Find the one big thing you want to be famous for with customers, a difference that will make their lives better in the most obvious way—then name it, frame it, and claim it.

- To get famous, stand for one thing: a difference that sets you apart and makes you the number one choice.
- That difference is the center of your Brand. A brand is your name with a specific reputation attached—the first idea customers think of
- That first idea must be a selling idea: it must be superlative, important, believable, measurable, and own-able.
- Brands aren't optional. Customers do it for you if you don't do it first.
- To build a brand that will make you famous, you must:
  - Name It
  - Frame It
  - Claim It
- Give your brand a four-line elevator pitch that everyone can remember and repeat.
- Remember, the idea you become famous for—that difference you name, frame, and claim—rallies your own team as much as it does your customers.

13

Everything You Need to Know about Creating Revenue, a.k.a. Selling (in about an Hour)

MARKETING WITHOUT SALES IS LIKE
MOTHERHOOD WITHOUT SEX

Ask any businessperson whether marketing is important, and they'll say yes, marketing is critical; a business needs marketing!

But why?

Because marketing is about bringing your products outside your own walls and into the world where customers live so you can offer them for sale. No sales, no revenue. No revenue, no business and no employees dressed in black in the marketing department.

So your business doesn't need marketing per se; what it *needs* is revenue, the monetary result of sales. We believe that nothing is more vital to your success as an entrepreneur than your ability to sell. And since this book is about the essence of entrepreneurial power, this chapter's going directly to the most important thing they don't teach at the elite business schools: *selling*. If you understand how it works, you'll get your marketing to do the work it's supposed to: make it easier for sales to produce the revenue you need.

As a great mentor put it simply, "Everything is selling." Beyond business, success in just about anything, from academia (winning those grants) to politics (attracting votes) or parenting (convincing your kids to do things your way) depends on it. When we pitch a new idea to our team, we are selling. When we try to persuade our children to do the right thing, we are selling. When we run for public office and speak to voters, we are selling. When we talk our friends into seeing the rerun of *Dirty Harry* and not the latest Dark Knight flick, we are selling. It is the number one active ingredient in capitalism. Nothing is more important to you as an entrepreneur or a valued team member than a practical understanding of the basic anatomy of sales.

Selling is simply this: *persuading another person to take a voluntary action*.

That means *any* action—from agreeing to invest in a business idea to going out with you on a date. Any feat of persuasion is a form of selling, whether you're a physician convincing a reluctant patient to have an operation, a politician seeking voter support for a new tax plan, or a car dealer moving a buyer into the driver's seat of a Subaru instead of the Toyota across the street. And it's the same whether you are talking to one person at a time or presenting to a group. Every time you persuade with a purpose, you are affirming the classic saying: "Everything in business comes down to selling."

As small children, we all start out as natural salespeople—just watch a four-year-old trying to talk his mother into buying him an ice cream cone. It's time to recapture that natural selling instinct. When you master the five sequential steps described below (along with the sixth emotional one), you will be more successful at everything in your life—starting with entrepreneuring.

Selling is nearly always required to make things happen because human beings don't like to change, period, even when it's in their best interests. They don't like to move from the safe spot they're in, make a decision, take a risk, or fix what isn't broken. Instinctively, we all default to "no" before "yes" because of that most ancient of all heuristics: "The one I know is the one that's safe."

So unless human beings are in active, acute pain—in which case they'll grab anything you give them to make it stop—they do not automatically want a better mousetrap or a better software solution for collaborative file sharing. They have other things to worry about. They think your new mousetrap is a pain in the butt.

Yet the lifeblood of your new business depends on getting people to volunteer to change—to try and to accept your new product. Only then will they hand you revenue and give you the chance to be a going business, one where revenue exceeds costs.

This requires sales. Those who disdain sales as crass and unpleasant, disdain success. They also don't understand it.

But the good news is that this attitude is easily fixed. Sales is the most teachable of all business skills. Anyone who pays attention to the simple, timeless steps we'll outline below can become good at it.

THE "SELLING IS EVIL" MYTH

The first step to proficiency in something is to debunk the false myths and negative perceptions that stand in our way. Nowhere is this more important than with selling. Ask any consumer the words that pop into his or her mind when they think about salespeople. You'll get words like *pushy, manipulative, obnoxious, untrustworthy, loud, phony, talkative* . . . and worse.

The traditional brand image of salespeople (made infamous by the brilliant David Mamet in his play *Glengarry Glen Ross*) is bad, to say the least. As a result, the average person is repelled by the idea of having to sell as part of their job because they think successful selling requires them to act that way.

Now here's what's fascinating. Ask that same consumer to describe the best sales experience and salesperson they ever had. They'll say, "She listened. She really cared about my needs. She gave me time to ask all my questions. She knew everything about the product and explained the pros and the cons. She really understood my problem. I felt comfortable."

Then ask whether they bought anything from that person. The answer is almost always, "Yes, of course, and I recommended her to my friends, too."

And then ask, "If you wanted to be a successful salesperson, which kind would you be?" It's a no-brainer. They'd be the listening, caring, trustworthy, helpful, and no-pressure kind. And so should you.

Contrary to popular myth, the most successful salespeople are never the backslapping fast talkers. They are the best listeners and the best at finding out the customer's real pain and concerns. For these reasons, they build trust with customers who come back to them over and over again, because they perform a critical service: they help their customers get off the fence of uncertainty, make decisions, and take action that's in their best interest.

Remember, people have that natural inertia, that natural tendency to avoid risk and stay put. The best salespeople help customers overcome their fear of decision making and change, so they can move forward. When customers make a choice and are satisfied, they love the salesperson for it.

The most successful people in the world get what they want by concentrating on first giving other people what *they* want. What other people want is to be listened to, cared about, made to feel important, able to trust someone—and then have their needs met. If you're able to listen, care, and help someone, you can be absolutely great at selling.

THE FIVE UNIVERSAL STEPS TO SELLING

Whether you are talking about person-to-person, face-to-face selling, relationship selling, organization selling, or any other new-age kind of selling from the latest seminar, the timeless sequence for selling never changes, no matter what names are put on it by what consultant.

Here that timeless sequence.

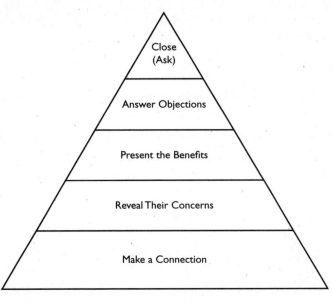

Figure 13.1   The Sales Pyramid

The Sales Pyramid is shaped this way for a reason: the size of each level of the pyramid is proportional to the importance and time you should spend on each step. You start at the bottom.

1. *Making a Connection* means approaching a customer, getting permission to interrupt their time and space so they might listen to what you are proposing.

2. *Revealing Their Concerns* means finding out this customer's true need, pain, or desire by asking a few questions, then listening a lot.

3. *Presenting the Benefits* means showing what is most relevant and interesting to the customer about your product based on the needs, pain, and concerns they've shared with you.

4. *Answering Objections* means responding to the final questions of assurance and clarification that *every buyer has to ask* before they can give themselves permission to buy.

5. *Closing* means asking for the order or asking them to take the next forward step in a complex buying sequence, like a

corporate sale that involves several layers of approval. No one buys until you ask.

All five steps are critical to the sale. But the great salespeople spend far more time and energy on those two wide steps at the bottom, because they know that will propel them directly to the top faster and with less effort. Getting the bottom two steps right makes the rest fall into place. Knowing this enables the best salespeople to say, "The sale was easy—the customers closed themselves."

Enthusiasm

Finally, there's that one emotional part we mentioned that goes with the other five. This is the part that little kids are so good at, even though they haven't taken a sales course by Dale Carnegie.[1] It's simply this: a genuine love and respect for your product and the sincere belief that it will improve the lives of anyone who buys it. This is what great salespeople call enthusiasm. This one element transfers trust and belief from your mind into the customer's mind, and that's the most important selling step of all. It allows even a rookie to get out there and sell with confidence. And it's the one thing you can't fake. If you don't have honest enthusiasm for your product, you must either fix the product or sell something else. Life is too short for you and your customers to do otherwise.

Using the Pyramid

We're not going to turn you into a super-salesperson in the next several pages. Most sales courses take at least a couple of days and require you to read a basic selling book. And, of course, as with any other skill, true mastery begins when you get wet—in this case,

---

[1]Dale Carnegie is often considered the father of modern-day sales training. His original classic, *How to Win Friends and Influence People*, still sells thousands of copies annually, 75 years after it was published. We recommend it to everyone. It's proof that the human principles behing selling (and lots of other key business activities) never change.

when you jump into the marketplace and start selling. But we can introduce you to the steps and ask you to take our word for it that mastering this simple sequence is the key to it all.

Once you get it, you'll also recognize when professional salespeople are going through the same sequence with you. You'll appreciate it when they do.

Important Note

We're going to assume the classic sales scenario in our examples because it's the most challenging. It's the kind where you initiate a conversation with a stranger, a qualified lead or prospect, who didn't ask to meet you first and probably has never heard of you. This is what any salesperson on the road, or any phone salesperson required to open new accounts, has to do. It's also what you have to do when you meet an attractive person at a club and decide to ask for a date, or when you show up at a county voters' caucus and present yourself as a candidate for the local legislature.

Even if you work in a clothing store or an auto dealership where interested people walk in looking for you, you'll still have to go through all the steps in the sequence to close the actual sale. You just won't have to do the cold-approach part. So we think everyone benefits from knowing the whole process start to finish.

1. Make a Connection

Our starting point is quite simple: you have to create a connection with another person to get permission to have the conversation that results in a sale.

When you approach a qualified customer for the first time, they are generally in the middle of doing something else. They are worried, anxious, or absorbed in their own issues. They are not interested in being interrupted by you unless you give them a good reason to be, very, very quickly. Once they're listening at all, you must get their permission to take their time to begin the sequence of selling. Remember, this is 100 percent voluntary.

There is one best way to break through this ice: you must use an *approach question*. The approach question puts an important proposition in front of a customer so fast and so convincingly that she only has one reasonable response: "What is it?"

The following is our all-time favorite approach question. If you use only this question in your entire sales career, you'll still be successful. It's a work of art:

"If there was a way for me to *lower your phone bill by at least 50 percent*, while *doubling your network*, you'd want to know about it, wouldn't you?[2]

As you can see, we've italicized a few words that are specific to a particular product. Depending on the product you sell, you'll modify those words to fit the situation and to capture your DSI.

You can see what this question does. It implies in an nanosecond that you may have something specific and valuable to give the customer. You've instantly transformed annoyance into curiosity. In a moment, the customer is asking you to tell her more about your product.

We've all had call center people who have never been taught this fundamental rule interrupt us just as we've sat down for dinner. They've been instructed by their supervisors to sound pleasant and friendly, so their first question is: "How are you doing today?"

For most people, the true response would be, "Rotten, you just spoiled my dinner." Click. The only way for a salesperson to get through would be with an instant approach question that forces the listener to ask, "What is it?"

We have another motive in giving you this specific example. We want you to see that the art of selling has a real method to it that's been honed and practiced for thousands of years. There are concrete techniques you can learn very quickly to turn yourself into a far better persuader and negotiator than you are now. No matter what you choose as a career, from politics to parenting, these selling skills will make you better at it.

---

[2]This is the great approach question taught by the international Dale Carnegie Sales Course.

So the first key step is to get permission to engage another person at all. If you engage *without* permission, it's called harassment.

Once you've made an initial connection, you must start to build *rapport*. Rapport is the beginning of comfort and trust with another person.

Rapport does not mean being liked, which is the second great misperception in selling. Because the fact is that *people don't buy from people they like, they buy from people they trust.* Being liked never hurts, of course, but you don't have to get someone to want to have a beer with you to persuade them they will benefit by owning your product.

Again, there are whole branches of psychology and books written on how to create instant rapport with others. Many success gurus, including Tony Robbins, have advocated various techniques, like Neuro-Linguistic Programming—the process of consciously getting in sync with another person's unconscious pace of movement, cadence, and volume of speech to make them feel "she's like me."

There are probably grains of truth in these theories. What we'll say is this: genuine friendliness, a genuine smile, genuine good manners, and a genuine interest in helping another person understand a benefit you sincerely believe in have never diminished anyone's chances of creating rapport with another human being.

You have one job now in the sales process: to get to step 2—to get your customers to reveal their concerns.

2. Reveal Their Concerns

The best listeners always make the best salespeople. The reason is simple: if you ask people questions about themselves, then you shut up and listen, they *will tell you.* They will tell you how they feel, what they want and need, what pains them, and what they prefer. They will feel more rapport with you the more they talk because being listened to makes them feel valued and grateful. Sometimes they realize feelings or needs they didn't even know they had. But this is certain: the more people talk to you, the more they will tell you exactly how they like to buy and exactly what you need to do to sell your product to them.

The big, loud sales talkers barrel in and try to crack the safe open by blowing it up with dynamite. The great listeners let their customers drop the keys to the safe right in the palm of their hand. That's why, contrary to popular myth, the best salespeople aren't the closers, they are the openers.

The basic way to get customers to reveal their concerns is to remember the Six Honest Serving Men. These are the so called open-ended questions, the kind that have to be answered with information, not a simple yes or no. Use them again and again to peel back the layers until you approach the real heart of the issue. Here's a little rhyme that will help you remember them:

There are six honest serving men, they tell me all I know,

Their names are *what* and *why* and *who* and *where* and *when* and *how*.

If you practice using these words to create open-ended questions, you can easily become a psychiatrist and charge people $600 per hour to sit on your couch and tell you all their concerns. It works like Lego: you just keep attaching one open-ended question onto the back of another until you get to what really matters to them: "What happened? And how did that make you feel? And why do you think you did that? And how would you feel if that happened? And then, how would you feel if *that* happened? I see. Okay then, our time is up for today. Six hundred dollars, please."

Getting customers to reveal their concerns isn't a whole lot different. Once they've told you about their real wants, fears, and needs, you can zero in directly on those needs in step 3.

3. Present the Benefits

Now you present your stuff. This is where you lay down your DSI and your product's key supporting features and benefits.

The difference between features and benefits is simple and important:

A *feature* is what it is: four-wheel disk brakes, a leather-trimmed radio, a six-inch shag carpet.

A *benefit* is "why I need it," why I should care: the brakes let you stop *before* you hit the other car; the leather-trimmed radio actually lets you smell the country and western songs while you listen; the six-inch shag carpet makes your car feel like a man cave when you drive to the local tavern with your buddies.

You should always tailor the features and benefits you describe to the needs revealed by your customer. Why, for example, did we mention the leather-trimmed radio? Because the customer spent 10 minutes telling us about his love for C&W music and that he loves to cruise around El Paso with his friends on Saturday nights. We know this because we asked about the customer's concerns and interests before the pitch, and he told us his hot buttons.

This is the most important advantage you can get in personal selling and you never want to waste it. By listening and finding out individual preferences, you can *tailor your DSI to that customer* on the fly—you can emphasize the key attributes that matter to that person most. This is an advantage that no mass-market advertiser who has to appeal to 50 million people in a 30-second Super Bowl commercial will ever have.

4. Answer Objections

As all serious buyers get closer to "yes," they raise objections.

Amateur sellers get nervous and afraid when this happens. But professionals *love* objections. They know an objection means they are right on the threshold of the sale. It's the customer asking for his own permission to buy, and asking you for help in making the decision. An honest objection is also an indication of the customer's trust in you as the seller because she is sharing her real, final fears and concerns about going forward and handing you the opportunity to sweep these fears away.

Knowing that objections are key to the psychological sequence of buying, professionals are calm and ready when they come. By exposing the objections to the sunlight of information, they can help the buyer see them fully, correct any misunderstandings, overcome final reluctance, and reduce the chances of buyer's remorse the day after. They know every objection is an opportunity to turn a perceived negative into a positive. In so doing, the final barriers evaporate, leaving the buyer content—even eager—to say yes.

What throws off professional salespeople is not an objection, it's *no* objection or a hidden objection that the buyer won't share. When a buyer wants to "come back later," "needs to check with his spouse," or "will consider it along with the other bids," he is not objecting (i.e., continuing the conversation), he's telling you he'd like you to stop and go away. At this point, a professional either asks directly for the customer's hidden objection—"Jack, it would help me to know: what's the real reason you've decided not to go ahead today?"—or leaves politely because this selling opportunity is over.

Learn to love objections. They're not obstacles; they are your opportunity to close the sale.

Great salespeople have discovered there's a method to handling objections that can be practiced and applied by anyone who wants to learn. When a customer voices an objection, she wants to (1) be listened to, (2) feel that she is understood, and (3) think that her concern is fair and sensible. Then she'll open herself to the answers you give back.

There are classic templates for handling objections that are so well known, they have names. They are often taught in sales training because they're simple and effective.

The most famous is called "Feel, Felt, Found." It automatically acknowledges the concern, makes the customer feel reasonable, and only then offers a gentle counterpoint, proven by others, all contained in a little story. After listening intently, the salesperson says:

"Mr. Jones, I know how you *feel*. Many of our best customers *felt* exactly the way you did when they first saw our solution. But then when they tried it, they *found . . .*"

- ". . . they saved 50 percent on their phone bills and got better service.
- ". . . our composite material was stronger, more dent-resistant, and lasted twice as long as aluminum.
- ". . . the extra $2 they were paying per unit doubled the number of click-throughs and conversions that followed."

Again, the reason to demonstrate a script like this is to show you how straightforward and easy to apply the techniques of effective selling can be.

There are dozens of other ways to answer objections (although we think that "Feel, Felt, Found" is an excellent one). But the underlying psychology remains the same. You must listen, acknowledge, empathize, and then show how the customer's (valid) concern will be cancelled out by the benefits.

5. Close (Ask)

Closing means asking—requesting that a customer take the action that will get them the desired benefit. It's asking for the order.

Closing strikes fear and loathing into salespeople and customers alike because it's the term most associated with the pushy, aggressive, obnoxious salesperson who always seems to be pressing customers to buy what they don't need or want to do. When a salesperson closes too aggressively or prematurely, customers will pay good money just to get him to go away. This type of selling doesn't just turn customers off, it keeps nice people from going into selling because they think they'll have to behave this way.

But once again, the opposite is true. The hard closer is simply trying to go straight to step 5, without going through steps 1 through 4
of the pyramid.

The person who understands the first four steps—who makes
a connection and starts building rapport and trust, helps the
customer reveal his concerns and needs, presents a solution
tailored to those needs, and then responds convincingly to the
remaining objections—never needs to push, force, or pressure
the prospect. By the time it's time to close, the prospect is already
sold. Now all that's left for this seller to do is to simply, calmly
and confidently, ask.

As painless and nondramatic as this kind of closing will be, there
is still no getting around the fifth step. As long as we are selling to
humans, if you want someone to take an action, you have to ask. It's
as simple as that.

In recent decades, a whole genre of sales books and programs
have appeared that are dedicated to the notion that closing is obsolete in the new age, so you don't have to trouble yourself or the
prospect with this final step.

Sorry, but it just ain't so. If you're not sure whether to believe us,
consider this. A young man and woman in love may have the world's
most tender relationship, the ultimate in rapport and trust. They may
be 100 percent ready to spend the rest of their lives together. But
unless one of them, one day, stops and simply asks the other, "Will
you marry me?," the marriage never happens. Somebody *still* has to
close.

If it takes asking to accomplish a sale like that, it's hocus pocus to
think you don't need to close when you're asking a stranger to hand
you his money. It has to be done—but it doesn't have to hurt. If you
learn and practice the Five Steps, it almost never will.

Classic Closing Techniques   No step in the sales process has been
more analyzed, discussed, or written about through the ages than
closing. Some of the closing gambits are so classic, they even have
names: "The Order Book Close," "The Door Knob Close," "The

Puppy Dog Close," "The Assumptive Close," and maybe the most famous, "The Ben Franklin Close."[3]

As with the Feel, Felt, Found script or the Dale Carnegie approach question, these closing techniques are just structured bits of psychology that can help salespeople get proficient in a skill set quickly, using proven templates.

You can find these classics in any traditional sales course. They're kind of fun to learn. Yet they all come down to the one thing you need to remember: When it's time to make the sale, you must simply and plainly *ask*. Your prospect wants and needs to be asked.

Ask and ye shall receive.

THE X FACTOR IN SELLING

The X factor is your enthusiasm—the feeling you project directly from your own love, trust, and belief in your own product. There is the emotional piece that powers the most successful sellers and persuaders. It trumps just about everything else.

This mastery comes built in to anyone who was ever a three-year-old. Enthusiasm is your natural gift and advantage. If you don't love your product and everything it stands for—and you don't want the whole world to share your enthusiasm—find another product.

TEACH YOURSELF TO SELL THE ACCELERATED PROFICIENCY WAY

The finer points of sales training are beyond the scope of this chapter, but if there was ever a subject already packaged and available for Accelerated Proficiency, sales is it. You and every member of

---

[3]In the Ben Franklin Close, the salesperson says, "When old Ben Franklin got to decision time, he used to pull out a sheet of paper and draw one line down the middle. On one side he'd list all the reasons against. On the other he'd list all the reasons for. It was easy to make the right decision, once he could look at the pros and cons like that. The side that was greatest, won." The salesperson pulls out a sheet, draws the line, and asks the prospect to list as many reasons for and against as he can. He might remind him of a few additional ones they'd agreed on. Then he asks, "What do you think we should do?" If the salesperson has done his job, the positive side nearly always wins.

your team should read one or two of the great books on selling; listen to one of the great CDs that are available by the great trainers like Brian Tracy and the legendary Zig Ziglar; or take a short, high-quality sales course, preferably one not longer than a couple of days. Then get out in the marketplace and start selling.

You really can teach yourself to sell in an accelerated amount of time by studying and applying the lessons offered in these short, entertaining works by the masters of selling. You will get it after that, and you will never look at persuasion, presentations, or even negotiations the same way again.

HOW MUCH REVENUE? JUST BREAK EVEN

Let's come back to what selling exists to do: generate the revenue for your enterprise.

As an entrepreneurial founder, you'll need to think ahead and plot your basic plan: (1) Who is going to buy from you (that is, who is your target market)? (2) How much do you need to sell them to cover your costs? (3) How much money, development, and time will you need to get yourself to market so selling can actually begin?

Don't make your plan complicated. Don Valentine, one of the founders of Sequoia Capital, the famous VC firm, once said, "Your business plan should be able to fit on the back of a business card." He was exaggerating slightly, but he made his point. Don Valentine had just been pitched too many business plans that were six months in the making and took hours to present, but couldn't clearly answer the basic questions, "What is it? Why do I need it? Who's going to buy it? How much cash do we need to get started? And how much time, money, and staff will it take for us to *break even?*"

Breaking even is the goal line, folks. Crossing it is the magic moment when your business becomes a living thing. It's the moment the plane flies, the aspiring surfing stands up straight on the board, and the homing pigeon makes it home. It means having enough customers buying from you to sustain a business that sells enough to cover all of its costs, including yours and your teammates', day after day, month after month. It is the first, great milestone in any UnStoppable company's success.

Your mission from day one is to focus on reaching this revenue moment.

After that, you're off to the races.

- Marketing without sales is like motherhood without sex.
- The rules of selling are simple, straightforward, and fun. Learn them and have everyone in your company learn them.
- The best salespeople are the best listeners, not talkers.
- The Five Steps of Selling are:
  - Make a Connection
  - Reveal Their Concerns
  - Present the Benefits
  - Answer Their Objections
  - Close (Ask)
- The enthusiasm that comes from belief in your business trumps every other skill in selling.
- Your revenue plan is to "just break even." Focus all your efforts from day one reaching that goal.

14

Everything You Need to Know about Perfecting Your First Product (in about an Hour)

PROFESSIONALS MAKE IT REAL, NOT IDEAL

The product you sell is the last element of the UnStoppable Six. As we've noted, to avoid having to say "product and/or service" every time, we just use the word *product* to describe what customers pay you to give them—because product and service are, in essence, the same.

Notice that we've saved this section for last. Popular myth says that product comes first—that entrepreneurs spend all their time dreaming up a million-dollar idea like the Frisbee or bifocal lenses, then patent it, and then start raking in profits. The underlying assumption is that the product is fail-safe at conception—which implies that the would-be entrepreneur should think first and foremost about product.

But by now you may smell a paradox coming. The odds of success are stacked with a vengeance against those who try to launch a business the "perfect it first," product-centric way. Instead, you must think about every element in the UnStoppable Six from day one, then build a Minimum Viable Product (MVP) that provides the benefit you assume customers need for a price they can afford. You must put this actual, *imperfect* test product into their hands as soon as you possibly can so they can see, touch, wear, drive, or otherwise use it. Then listen, learn, and adjust as *customers* tell you how to transform your flawed product into the ideal, million-dollar baby that everyone wants to buy.

Remember how we said the best salespeople aren't the best talkers, they're the best listeners? Well, the same goes for entrepreneurs developing their first product. The most successful ones are the best listeners. They live by this credo:

"If you listen to what customers tell you about the real pluses and minuses of your product, they will give you the keys to the safe."

REMEMBER, NOBODY WANTS 57 FEATURES; THEY WANT 1 DONE BEST

We first covered this rule in Chapter 6 (Ideas, People, and Execution), but it's so important, it's worth hearing it explained by someone who lives it every day.

We spoke recently to Nick Longo, a seasoned, successful entrepreneur and cofounder and director of Geekdom in San Antonio, Texas. Geekdom is a collaborative workspace started by Rackspace founders, where entrepreneurs, developers, and innovators can meet potential team members, share, learn, and work every day for a small monthly membership fee in a community atmosphere. Geekdom's mission is to seed and feed new entrepreneurs in the San Antonio metro area, expand the entrepreneurial ecosystem, and grow new employers like Rackspace for the city at large.

Nick sees a *lot* of new product ideas every day. We asked if he recommends any books or classes on developing the idea and first prototype for fledgling products.

"You don't need a book," he said. "Just a few principles I can tell you right now before my cell coverage cuts out in the parking garage." Needless to say, we like the set of this man's sails. So what follows is a paraphrase of the product wisdom we learned from Nick Longo.

Feature Creep Kills

The biggest rookie mistake is feature creep. You see this problem especially with geeks and software developers who love their gadgets, but it applies to everyone. They work for months to "enhance" and "improve" their product, creating minor feature after feature, thinking they need more and more. But what they really need to do is find the one thing their product will do better than anyone else's—something the customer needs and will pay for—and get a test product to market ASAP. Otherwise, you may be working for months on a product that nobody wants, or one that customers might want if you fix something basic that you couldn't see.

The only way to find out is to complete your MVP and get it out there. Customers have no bias or ax to grind. They will tell you the truth fast. Customer feedback is worth its weight in gold, and we never stop reminding entrepreneurs of its importance.

Sometimes customer feedback makes you realize the need to fold your tent on this particular idea and move on. Even so, you *always* learn something of great value from any test product that you can put into your next product idea. You haven't failed, you've pivoted. You've opted to move in a better direction. Other times, customers give you the golden nugget you didn't see that makes your current idea a winner. And if you're listening to customers, it's really common to find that the feature you thought was the main thing isn't what they love about your product at all. What they love is a side function you thought was a throwaway, but they can't get enough of it. They're telling their friends about it. By accident, they've shown you a really *big* need and desire, which leads to the product feature and benefit on which you should be focusing your business.

The "And versus Or" Rule

We also tell entrepreneurs to change their mind-set from "and" to "or" because choosing the big focus of your product is usually a choice of this versus that, a series of sacrifices, not a pileup of additives that annoys most customers. We tell them, " 'And' doesn't scale. The secret is 'Or.' "

The "30–60–90" Rule

Another rule of thumb we give every developer is to think 30–60–90. The 30–60–90 rule applies specifically to web app developers, but it's relevant for any new product, from a restaurant or hair salon to a line of homemade jams and jellies.

1. *By Day 30, Build It.* That is, take it from an idea to a three-dimensional MVP—a tangible product that you can demonstrate and that someone else can see, try, and experiment with. It won't be close to perfect, but its critical parts must work and it must be able to perform what you've promised, more than once. This is where the founders do the first dry runs to see if it really works or if the developer is just smoking it.

2. *By Day 60, Validate with Customers.* You take the MVP and try it out with people, recording notes all the way and adjusting where you can. The key here is to also do a "private beta" with just a few of your most trusted friends and mentors. They'll take the time to give you deeper feedback. You want this phase to be limited and controlled because your product still has serious bugs and you don't want it going into the world and getting panned before it's ready for prime time.

3. *By Day 90, Release Version 1.0—the Public Beta.* Your company still calls this a beta, but it's a much more public release. You're still going to be fixing problems and customer issues, but now you're getting proof of concept before a much wider audience—like the way Broadway shows used to "open out of town," in theatres in Boston or Philadelphia, before facing the make-or-break judgment of the critic from *The New York Times*. (The addition or revision of a few songs or scenes between New Haven and the Great White Way spelled the difference between flop and hit for more than one classic musical.)

The 30–60–90 Rule forces entrepreneurs to act by imposing real, numerical deadlines for getting the thing out there and into customers' hands where it belongs.

"Minimum Viable" Means Not Too Soon

Minimum and *viable* are two words to take literally when it comes to developing and testing your MVP. They mean just what they say. Yes, you can have people test-drive your super-handling experimental car before you've finished choosing the paint scheme or even installing the back seats—but you can't do it before the engine can start, the gears can shift, and you can drive fast around the track. By the same token, you can open your motel before the outside landscaping is finished, but not before you have bedsheets and shower curtains.

MVP means you have to be able to demonstrate your DSI in performance before making a promise and exposing yourself to customers. If you test too soon, you waste the prospect's time and risk your credibility, and often you won't get a second chance.

This happens too often with new restaurants. The local community has been waiting for the new eatery to open for months. The menu looks fun and everyone's hoping a great new place has been added to the town. It's packed the first night. But the problem is that opening night is about a week too soon. The wait staff is slow and confused. The orders get mixed up. The chicken tenders are undercooked. The credit card machine isn't connected and someone from the table has to go out to an ATM to get cash. The manager runs around apologizing: "This is our first week, you know." Most people are sympathetic—they're just not in the mood to ever come back. You've asked them to sacrifice a chunk of their monthly dining budget to be your guinea pigs. Worse, they will tell their friends.

This business simply opened before it had an MVP: delicious hot food, served reasonably quickly in a pleasant atmosphere.

Restaurants offer an extreme case, but if you burn first-time triers by failing on your core promise, (1) you won't get an accurate test of how your product performs with customers, and (2) those prospects may never return. That's a fatal first mistake if you're a local business.

So get to market soon, but don't serve the cake until it's baked. Recognizing the difference takes judgment and the willingness to listen to your gut instincts. An entrepreneur needs both.

———

WHICH DATA TO LISTEN TO, WHICH TO THROW AWAY?

Here's the big question about products. We know that people resist change of any kind and are natural doubters, especially when it comes to other people's new ideas. And we know that many people (especially your friends) want to be nice when you show them a prototype you've slaved over for months, so they're likely to say nice things. But you need the truth. How do you decide whether feedback should be taken to heart or ignored?

It's a judgment call if you only have a small universe of test customers, but here's a helpful rule of thumb. A person who simply tells you, "It's awesome, dude," is just being courteous. If she starts *using* your product after the trial, she's a satisfied user. And if she *tells others* about it, and particularly if she's interested enough to engage you and talk about it, in all likelihood she'll become a real customer or, even better, a promoter.

On the other hand, few people outside of family and friends will take the time or trouble to tell you how they really feel if they don't like your product. They'd rather just move on, usually without volunteering any concrete explanation.

But it's worth your while to try to discover the real reason, even when that requires a bit of probing. When you can engage the group who didn't buy and find out the real reasons why your product didn't work for them, it's often the most valuable feedback you'll ever get.

The other rule of thumb is that if you want real, honest positive and negative feedback (the only kind you want) about your beta, you've got to mean it when you ask for it. People will know if you're sincere and be much more likely to tell you the truth.

Sometimes the nature of your product makes it relatively easy to capture feedback from a large number of users. For example, if you have a downloadable app, which affords a bigger beta universe, you can avail yourself of wider-scale e-mail or Web surveys to reach people outside the walls of the compound. You'll still have to use your judgment to determine what the results really mean, and you'll always have a few outliers—angry, unreasonable naysayers on one side and a few people who will over-praise you on the other. Just capture all the data and learn from the trends.

Here some other basics on tapping the free genius of customers who are waiting to help perfect your MVP:

1. *Create a Feedback Loop*. First off, you need to get the data. Set up a feedback loop with friends, family, or with online surveys. You have to track and organize what you capture for it to teach you anything, especially when you are dealing with larger numbers.

2. *Question-and-Answer Quality, Not Quantity; Test Fewer Variables*. Remember, too much data makes you dumber. *A very small number of very important questions is always better than a barrage.* The rule is to reduce your variables to get the most meaningful test results. We're talking about three to five questions here. The answers to a monster questionnaire will overlap and confuse you as much as the respondents. We see this mistake all the time in even the biggest corporate marketing departments. If you want answers, not piles of pages, avoid making your survey an encyclopedia.

   The two most important questions we've ever found that yield the highest value when answered sincerely, are:

   a. Would you recommend this product to a friend or a colleague?

   b. Why or why not? (Write down the verbatims).

   This happens to be the basic couplet for the Net Promoter Score survey they've used for years at Rackspace, which we talked about in Chapter 11 (Everything You Need to Know about Succeeding with Customers (in about an Hour)).

3. *Adapt and Retry. Repeat: Adapt and Retry.* When you and your fellow founders get over your grief for one beloved feature or another that customers ignore or hate, fix it. Then you'll need a way to measure whether results have improved or not. Here is another awesome new advantage that is built

into tech entrepreneurship, especially web-based software development: there are free, off-the-shelf tools for tracking and measuring just about any activity and change in usage you'd want to measure.

―――――――

UNSTOPPABLE THEMES

The big unifying themes of *The UnStoppables* should be coming together for you as we complete our analysis of the UnStoppable Six. As the guy who runs Geekdom every day affirmed, "Simple wins," "Find a Dominant Selling Idea," "Focus most on what customers want and let them to *tell you* how to succeed," "Nobody knows anything—the market is always smarter than you are," and above all, "Get your product into *motion*." It's the same way that you must get yourself and your founders into motion. Motion is what makes magic.

This short chapter has been about what to aim for to create a unique, sellable product, not coming up with the "what" itself. The "what" germinates like a seed with a yearning, an inkling, an interest, or an unscratched itch. Then you apply the magic of the UnStoppable Six as you think about Difference, Team, what Customers want, whether there's a market you can sell to, if you can build it, and so forth. You think about these things—and work and rework them—over and over with your founders until an idea forms that you can't wait to execute.

In this game, the way to win a giant jackpot is to master the fundamentals, not to play the lottery—fundamentals like building an MVP, achieving the milestone of breaking even, and formulating an idea that has one obvious, appealing benefit rather than 30.

From pro athletes to the Navy SEALs, the greatest practitioners do one thing better than everyone else in the world: they are incredibly good at the fundamentals and they never stop practicing to master them. They know that the fundamentals are the gateway to all great things because the fundamentals are the essence. The more you practice conceiving and honing MVP, failing, succeeding, and failing until customers say it's right, the sharper your intuition will get, the better your judgment will be, and the more everything you touch will eventually turn to gold.

- Make it real, not ideal.
- You'll get a better product by being Triangle-centric, not product-centric.
- Feature creep kills. Do one thing best.
- Focus on "or" not "and."
- Stick to "Minimum Viable" in the strictest sense.
- Create a feedback loop, ask a few vital questions, then adapt and retry.
- Success comes down to the fundamental Unstoppable themes.

PART III

Conclusion
Us

15

Entrepreneur Country and the E-Companies

WE'RE BACK SITTING IN that little cafe in Tel Aviv, conversing with master entrepreneur Yossi Vardi.

"This is a whole country in motion," Vardi is telling us. We've seen it in action, so we know what he means. And we've seen the same principles at work in many other settings—in garages and labs in Silicon Valley, in collaborative incubators like Geekdom, in still-growing companies like Rackspace, and even among the high-powered, life-or-death teams shaped by the Navy SEALs. It's the spirit of mission, innovation, and achievement that animates Israel—a tiny country that lives in a very rough neighborhood on the global map, one where falling behind and ceding your leadership to others is not an option.

This little nation has one big thing going for it: abundant entrepreneurial anxiety. Israel has mobilized itself into an entrepreneurial and innovation powerhouse as a sheer matter of survival.

But what about the original start-up nation? Are our choices here in the United States so different?

THE STAKES ARE THE SAME

Jim Clifton, chairman and CEO of Gallup, offers a pretty stark answer to that question in his 2011 book *The Coming Jobs War*. He points out that as the unmatched economic leader since World War II, our nation not only has military authority, it has the moral authority to lead the world away from the worst regimes and toward democratic rights, to promote a better world. But, he says, "if the United States allows China or any other country or region to out-enterprise it, out-job-create it, out-grow its GDP, everything changes."

In other words, today's competition to build the strongest economy and the best jobs may not be a violent conflict like those that have convulsed the planet in the past—but if we were to lose, its outcome would feel the same. This one's for all the marbles. And right now, the trends aren't good. Clifton reports that in 2011, the U.S. GDP was almost $15 trillion and China's was $6 trillion. (Russia's was $1.47 trillion, and India's was $1.43 trillion). The median household income in the United States is about $51,000, compared to $10,000 in China. But China is coming on like a freight train. The difference is GDP growth. We're growing at 2 percent; China is growing at 10 percent. Simple math tells us what to expect: 6 trillion compounding over 30 years at 10 percent blows away $15 trillion compounding at 2 percent over the same period. So unless something changes in that timeframe, China will become the world's leading economy by a wide margin.[1]

The only reasonable course is to respond in proportion to the threat—to mobilize ourselves on a vast level all across our society, to go all in with our people and resources to remain winners in this grand arena.

We must do whatever it takes to maximize and mobilize our greatest legacy and our future hope: our entrepreneurs.

---

[1] Jim Clifton, *The Coming Jobs War* (New York: Gallup Press, 2011).

HOW WE CAN DO IT

A National Goal

This must become a full-blown national priority, as any true war effort would be. We need political and business leaders who can rally their constituents to a national entrepreneurial cause, and who want to make sure, as Tom Friedman of the *New York Times* has put it, that America remains the Cape Canaveral of start-ups in the globalization age. That means the subject isn't just inserted as an applause line every year in a State of the Union speech; it's declared as a national mission the way John F. Kennedy pointed to the moon and challenged the whole nation to go there.

The 10–10–10 Plan

Here's a goal worthy of JFK's call to land a man on the moon. We'll be electrified when we see the president of the United States stand, point upward, and say:

"We hereby commit as a nation to *doubling* our number of entrepreneurs by the end of this decade—those citizens who choose entrepreneurship as a career and help create new businesses, the great American engine of leadership and prosperity since the dawn of the Republic. Those people who have the dream and then dare to follow it will be patriots and heroes of a new generation."

No one agrees on the exact number of natural-born, normally occurring entrepreneurs in our workforce, but our best estimate is that it's around 10 percent. The behavioral scientists we spoke to said it'd be reasonable to tap another 10 percent, the ones who have simply lacked the access, the exposure, or the environment of entrepreneurship but who have the capacity that just needs to be effectively switched on. Ten years is an aggressive but plausible timeframe if we're committed enough; hence 10–10–10.

Since it's generally accepted that over 80 percent of all new jobs are created by businesses between one and five years old—those started by our current crop of entrepreneurs—we can confidently say that tapping an additional 10 percent would create a very large number of new jobs and new opportunities in this country.

A New Cabinet Post

We need a Cabinet-level Department of Entrepreneurship that is funded, staffed, and given the same status as a Department of Homeland Security or a Department of Education. This is necessary if our leaders believe, as more and more Americans do, that this mission is vital to the country.

There is precedent for it around the world. Israel has an Office of the Chief Scientist, who oversees the public-private partnership that has been crucial to the nation's start-up miracle. The office monitors the vital circuit between academia, research, and industry; it's also involved in incubator programs and in nurturing innovation that may be too undeveloped for private investment. The Office of the Chief Scientist doesn't favor any particular business category; it lets merit and the market decide where the support goes. It doesn't keep an investment stake or influence any company's decision-making. It exists solely to advance the nation's entrepreneurial prospects and economic health.

This is not the only example of smart, public-private entrepreneurial partnership at the highest levels of government. It shouldn't be framed as socialism or unwarranted government intrusion any more than what happened during both World Wars, when our government took a huge role in converting industries to wartime production. What we're talking about is teamwork between the private and public sectors, aimed at achieving the great national mission of our time.

And the fact is that our most aggressive competitors are fully engaged in business-building government partnerships. If you need an example, start with China.

THE ENTREPRENEURIAL GROUNDSWELL IS HAPPENING

The great news is that we are awakening. Entrepreneurial awareness is blooming in new initiatives and institutions all over the country. Accelerated mentoring and seed-financing organizations like

Y Combinator and TechStars are holding three-month sessions in major cities from San Jose to San Antonio to Boston that have helped launch hundreds of start-ups. Weekend entrepreneur boot camps, like 3 Day Startup for university students, are catching fire. Collaborative workspaces that let entrepreneurs move out of Starbucks and into a community working environment are popping up everywhere. In 2011, Rackspace's founders and friends got together and started Geekdom, a collaborative workspace in San Antonio. Geekdom is expanding so fast, it just moved into a new 45,000-square-foot space. It also hosts events and practical business classes, and houses an annual session of TechStars.

Entrepreneurship education is also moving into some of our charter schools, which should be seen as the tip of a very encouraging iceberg. It's never too early to expose kids to the entrepreneurial mind-set. We must help a new generation reframe their idea of work and think of themselves not just as job seekers, but as job creators.

TEACHING TO THE ESSENCE

Perhaps most important, we need to bring the techniques of emotional mechanics and Accelerated Proficiency from the isolated corners where they exist now—typically in specialized areas like military and sports training—into the mainstream curriculums where they don't yet exist. If MBA programs are going to teach entrepreneurship, they can no longer deny the need to expose their students to the essence that powers it. The educational establishment must accept that it's as critical a responsibility to teach students how to succeed in the face of fear, risk, and failure as it is for them to take tests and write term papers. It's as important to teach kids to lower the barriers that stop them as it is to teach the science, math, and other skills they need to know once they've unstuck themselves and put themselves in motion.

We're not merely proposing an additional course in high school. We're proposing a philosophical sea change in today's school systems, in which teachers have to get three permissions from the principal's office and have a medical aide standing by just to take the kids outside for a class on a nice June day.

Bringing emotional mechanics into the mainstream goes beyond the scope of this book, but it's not a pipe dream. The theory and practice behind it is well understood and has been taught quickly and efficiently in high-risk occupations for decades. Remember what whole societies can do and have done when faced with issues of survival in wartime. Educating our youth in emotional mechanics and reaping the benefits is only a matter of priority.

THE E-COMPANIES

Historian Will Durant once said that "before great civilizations are conquered from without, they are destroyed from within." It's the same for great companies. But any business that wants to compete in the new era by leaving none of its creativity, energy, enthusiasm, or commitment on the table can become the biggest engine of entrepreneurial mobilization there is, starting now. It's in their employees', customers', and shareholders' best interests to do so.

We know this because Rackspace has been building an entrepreneurial engine since 1998—a work forever in progress, up to about 5,000 people now and adding about 100 new people a month. Zappos.com, the legendary online shoe retailer (acquired by Amazon in 2009) and Google are also said to operate this way—large companies that have kept the entrepreneurial spirit alive.

We call such businesses *E-Companies*.

"E" of course stands for Entrepreneur, the element that is kept vibrant in such a company's DNA from its 1st day to its 10,000th day. These companies knowingly and proudly run on emotional mechanics because they understand entrepreneurial thinking and celebrate it at every level, from the CEO and founders who are the keepers of the vision, to the teammates "down on the floor" who are encouraged to see themselves as entrepreneurs working on the mission, not just employees working for the man. Everybody in an

E-Company believes in an articulable set of values that drive progress and decision making in the same direction.

Given what we've seen on our journey to write this book—and looking back on what the founders did at Rackspace based on their intuitive knowledge of these principles—we now know that the E-Company spirit carries human power of such limitless creativity and magnitude that any company that taps it will leave traditional companies in the dust. In the global tsunami of hyper-competition that's racing our way, only the E-Companies that harness this power will be able to compete.

One common trait of all E-Companies is the Belief Culture. That means they all:

- are built on a shared mission;
- manage to members' strengths;
- live on values that supersede any personal agenda;
- love customers;
- care about their team members; and
- trust implicitly that initiatives taken to advance these values—by innovating, stretching service, risking for the right reasons, and sometimes failing in order to learn—will never be punished by leaders because everyone is fighting for the same cause.

This is the culture what kicks and breathes inside the E-Company.

────────

FEAR CULTURES

Fear Cultures, on the other hand, are the old-fashioned, top-down, command-based kind of culture that dominated Western economies up until the digital age. In fear cultures, imperial C-level executives live on a palace floor, as far as possible from the noise and grit and low wages of the factory below. They manage by rooting out weaknesses, exposing and punishing mistakes, finding fault, cutting material and costs, and squeezing more and more efficient margins which usually squeezing quality and value as well. Fear Cultures compel humans to live in a protective rather than productive state at work. Employees in a fear-dominated organization know that risks and innovative thinking are too dangerous because failure is often punishable by (job) death.

Fear Cultures are designed to perpetuate a valuable status quo and demand conformity to traditional systems and standards. It's an approach to business that worked better s in an age of no or slow change—when companies could get established, dominate a category, and rest on laurels that the founding entrepreneurs provided for decades. Fear-based companies offered a reasonable quid pro quo that made workers' acceptance of politics and conformity reasonably worthwhile, because in return they used to provide some loyalty: the expectation of lifetime employment and a decent pension.

Not anymore.

Today these places are rife with managers and employees who stay because they're terrified of losing a job, not because they are getting the sense of mission and belonging that all human beings need from work. At the core, employees in command-and-control environments like these know deep down they are not trusted. In turn, they are cordial with but wary of their coworkers and managers.

But most important, employees in fear cultures can't mentally or physically serve customers with the kind of two-handed, all-in, cheerful commitment that the world increasingly demands. It's impossible to do this when you only have one free hand—because you need the other to protect yourself.

A work environment like this is seldom a happy place. And fear cultures by definition cannot be entrepreneurial. They are destined to be disrupted.

BELIEF CULTURES: HOW THEY HAPPEN

Remember Fish Camp in the chapter on true teams? The Aggies of Texas A&M live in a giant Belief Culture perpetuated for decades across hundreds of thousands of alumni. It starts with a firm superset of values that cover right and wrong, then it's codified in traditions, symbols, and language. It celebrates itself constantly, and always gives team members the benefit of the doubt. Action talks and bullshit walks in Belief Cultures. No one is held to a higher standard than leadership, which is why genuine middle management buy-in to the mission is the most critical challenge in an E-Company, especially as it scales. The Israeli Defense Force leaders consider this their biggest challenge as well. They also tell us that they can solve it only one way: by having midlevel officers serve the values, the big picture and the little picture, as much as top commanders.

Management sends signals through the ranks with every move they make, either upholding or betraying the code of values. Apple, for example, has long touted itself as a place where customers come first and employees matter. But certain recent actions may be challenging their Belief Culture, causing deep concern in customers, employees, and the press about whether Apple's corporate culture after Steve Jobs is remaining true to its entrepreneurial values.

One example was the summary destruction of billions of dollars' worth of customer-accessory attachments in a single stroke—with zero warning—by making all the old power cords obsolete in the new iPhones. Another was the attempt to forcibly eliminate Google Maps from the iOS platform and replace it with Apple's program, which didn't work. Management decisions like this not only would never be interpreted as putting customers first, but they also humiliate employees, who have to rationalize them to aggravated users and who as users are mad themselves.

We've also heard that corporate authorities took away a cherished symbol of trust and respect from the Apple Geniuses and other store team members when they stopped furnishing associates with the Customer Service Code. This is what had enabled any floor employee to escalate service levels and cancel charges without supervisors' permission, as long as their best judgment told them it was the right thing to do. Many former employees said they were heartbroken when this happened; it was a spirit-crushing move that told team members their leaders had slashed its investment in employee trust in order to increase profit at the world's highest market-cap company.

The belief tree is shaken when leadership does these kinds of things. It doesn't take too many hits for it to fall down.

MANAGING TO STRENGTHS

People measure what matters. Nothing has galvanized Rackspace's commitment to manage to people's strengths more than the company's decision to learn about and measure them, using the StrengthsFinder™ program, originally developed by Marcus Buckingham and Donald Clifton in their book, *Now Discover Your Strengths*. Since then, it's become a tradition for every team member at Rackspace to take the Strengths Test. Most display their five key strengths proudly for all to see, either emblazoned on their ID cards or somewhere on their desks.

Managing to strengths may be one of the simplest, most sensible philosophies ever developed to unleash human potential. It merely says that every person has natural strengths and weaknesses. When people work in a job that expresses their strengths, they are more energetic, creative, interested, passionate, and productive—effortlessly and happily so. However, the opposite is true when they are forced into jobs that run counter to their strengths. Thus, understanding and celebrating people's strengths, and doing whatever's possible to assign people to teams and tasks that support those strengths, makes talent flow with the grain, not against it.

At Rackspace, managing to strengths isn't just a nice idea—it's a real value that gets serious investment. By making every team member read the little book and take the short test to see which of the 36 named core strengths apply to them, Rackspace creates a shared language for regular discussions of the subject at any level in the company—a baseline that symbolizes the depth of the company's commitment to its people and to helping them maximize their individual talents for everybody's benefit. That's another characteristic strength of the E-Company.

NEW ENTREPRENEURS AND ENTERPRISES SPAWNED

Channeling human potential into entrepreneurial power is one of the greatest societal contributions E-Companies make. In fact, we think it's the patriotic duty of corporate citizens to get behind this war effort. Companies are by nature collaborative workplaces with lots of technical resources that bring together talented individuals. It's therefore natural in E-Companies for excited, empowered team members to bubble up with new ideas. Companies that sponsor entrepreneurial community development programs like Geekdom in San Antonio, and that encourage their own developers and makers to engage and mentor young entrepreneurs, more readily stimulate new product and business ideas, thereby helping the economy to grow and making the nation a better place for all of its citizens.

Some ideas will fit the mission of the parent company, while other will be spun off into new patents or business areas. But some need to leave the nest entirely because their destiny is to fly in a different direction.

When this happens, an E-Company doesn't see it as treason and call security to escort the offending entrepreneurs out the door. An E-Company is a birth mother. It is proud of the unique contribution it can make by spawning new offspring for our shared entrepreneurial future.

When entrepreneurs inside Rackspace develop an entrepreneurial idea of their own that is too powerful for them to deny, the company doesn't ask them to deny it. If their only choice is to follow this dream, then they go with the respect and blessing of their former colleagues. It's part of the DNA of Rackspace as an E-Company.

We know that people are hungry, even desperate to work in Belief Cultures that allow them to feel entrepreneurial. Once they've tasted it, they never want to go back. They literally love what work does in their lives; their loyalty to the company and what it stands for is fierce. They'll fight to protect it.

Several good books and articles on this topic have aimed to quantify how much more productive a company can be if it celebrates its customers, people, and values, as compared to the old-fashioned model. Author Stephen Denning, who calls the new style of management "Radical Management" and who has been studying the subject for years, claims that companies who operate this way are not just more profitable but hugely so, and that most of the legacy companies touted in Jim Collins's book, *Good to Great*, will go down the tubes if they don't change their ways. "It's not because the customers are more contented or because the people doing the work are happier or because it extends the life expectancy of a firm, generates jobs and fuels the growth of the economy," Denning says. "It does all those things, but the real driver of its inevitability is that it makes more money."[2]

There's no doubt that big, entrenched Fear Cultures with thousands of employees are hard to change. And we're not expecting the giant traditional corporations of the world to suddenly convert to E-Companies overnight; they've got a lot of baggage. The greatest hope is for the new entrepreneurial companies, the ones who embrace a different style of capitalism from day one. Call it Human Capitalism.

Every new enterprise is born as an E-Company, and it can stay that way so long as its people believe that what matters is to be a valued member of a winning team on an inspiring mission. At the rate these new companies are replacing the old guard, it won't take that long.

WELCOME TO THE ARENA

We want to leave you with the best quotation of them all. It could be titled "The Song of the Entrepreneur," but indeed it is a quotation from Theodore Roosevelt, repeated in a speech by President John F. Kennedy several decades later:

> The credit belongs to the man who is actually in the arena, whose face is marred by dust and sweat and blood, who knows the great enthusiasms, the great devotions, and spends himself in a worthy cause; who at best, if he wins, knows the thrills of high achievement, and, if he fails, at least fails while daring greatly, so that his place shall never be with those cold and timid souls who know neither victory nor defeat.

---

[2]Stephen Denning, *The Leader's Guide to Radical Management: Reinventing the Workplace for the 21st Century* (San Francisco: Jossey-Bass, 2010).

We hope this point in *The UnStoppables* marks a beginning for you, rather than an end. We hope that if there were to be only one take-away for you after spending your time with us, it would be this one:

You can't decide to be a visionary, or a genius, or to be particularly artistic, highly talented, or especially beautiful. You can't decide to have been born with money or a comfortable childhood or to have been sent to the best schools.

But you can decide this: To Dream, to Dare, and to Do. To stand with your fear and turn the struggle into your best advantage. To learn the essence, then get in motion.

There is one supreme thing in this life you get to decide.

You decide to become . . .

UnStoppable.

ACKNOWLEDGMENTS

IT TAKES A TRUE TEAM TO COMPLETE a project like this: partners, friends, mentors, teachers, and coworkers from several countries, companies, and schools past and present. We can only repay you all by paying it forward.

When we had the first inkling that our journey would take us through Israel, we had just two contacts: Joel Berkowitz of the American Technion Society and Robbie Greenblum, the Mayor of San Antonio's Chief of Staff, who had set up delegations to the Middle East in the past. There is only one degree of separation when it comes to introductions from folks like these; they really *do* know everybody! Technion Society members Charley Housen and Ed Goldberg—along with friend and liaison to the Mayor's Office, Roee Madai—also provided introductions that blossomed beyond any expectations. We want to thank (in the order of our meetings) Professor Dafna Schwartz, Chemi Peres, Yoram Yahav,

225

Yadin Kaufmann, Yoni Shimshoni, Professor Zehev Tadmor, Todd Dollinger, Arie Ovadia, Dr. Orna Berry, Yair Shamir, and Yossi Vardi.

Through Yossi, we were honored to meet Avi Hasson, Israel's Chief Scientist, and to take an unforgettable tour with Moshe Yanai. We want to thank Ya'acov Fried, who introduced us to Dr. Chaim Peri, founder of the Yemin Orde Youth Village, and to Col. Bentzi Gruber, director of the Ethics in the Field project. And we could never have accomplished our mission without being introduced to Yossef Idan, who guided us on pathways we never could have found, and who introduced us to friends like David Ouahnouna and other amazing teammates.

In Virginia Beach and San Diego, we were honored to meet and share the experiences and advice of active and retired U.S. Navy SEAL team members. Thanks first of all to Scott Chierepko, who organized the Virginia Beach roundtable (and simulated Oktoberfest) with Ed Maulbeck, Rob Smith, Bill Bickell, and Joseph Raetano (a veteran and friend of the group). Rob Roy and Surfer Kevin we thank for acquainting us with the BUD/S environment on the West Coast. Special thanks to Don Shipley and "Fuch" Fuciarelli for their personal generosity in introducing us to the power and emotion of live training at the Extreme SEAL Experience in Chesapeake, Virginia.

Last, but not least, we need to single out one old frogman in particular—Bill Seith—who has supported us with advice, anecdotes, fact checking, and editorial review on a weekly basis since the first days of the project. Thanks, Mug.

We are grateful for the inspiring words and observations about the True Team experience—from the most elite competitive levels, down to the everyday—from world champion formation skydivers and international coaches Dan Brodsky-Chenfeld, Mark Kirky, and Doug Park.

As for our publishers at John Wiley & Sons, Inc. we owe a debt to the person who seated us by chance next to Senior Editor Dan Ambrosio at the national entrepreneurial education conference in Washington, D.C. Dan gave us his business card, told us to keep in touch, and meant it. Thanks also to Christine Moore for her editorial encouragement, and to Lauren Freestone and Shannon Vargo for their skills and support.

Carlos Miranda must be called our Editor-at-Large for his cease-less dedication and his contributions on everything from data research to basic story structure, which he managed while writing his doctoral dissertation at Yale.

This brings us to friends, associates, and best-in-the-world assistants Sheryl Cruz and Celita Oman, who are there every day to offset any disorganized gene or impulse that might crop up with no advance warning.

Thanks to our UnStoppable entrepreneurial sounding boards Pat Condon, Lew Moorman, David Barnett, Nick Longo, Randy Smith, Dan Schley, Eric Jacobsen, M. Leo de Lion, and defender of the legal realm, Sara Dysart. Special mention also to Jason Carter, Cliff Barry, and John Fazio.

Down to the wire, we owe a permanent debt to our gold medal relay team, which carried us over the finish line: Lorenzo "The UnStoppable" Gomez, the great Bob Rivard, and the literary legend Karl Weber, editor extraordinaire.

The biggest embrace goes of course to our wives and our families—not only in this generation, but to parents and grandparents whose UnStoppable, creative, entrepreneurial spirits reside in us and without whom we never would have had the opportunity or the inspiration to write this.

And the final nod goes to all the people of Rackspace, the Rackers—who showed us how a big company really can keep its entrepreneurial spirit, and what it means to believe.

Warmest thanks to you all.

—Bill Schley

INDEX